AF584525

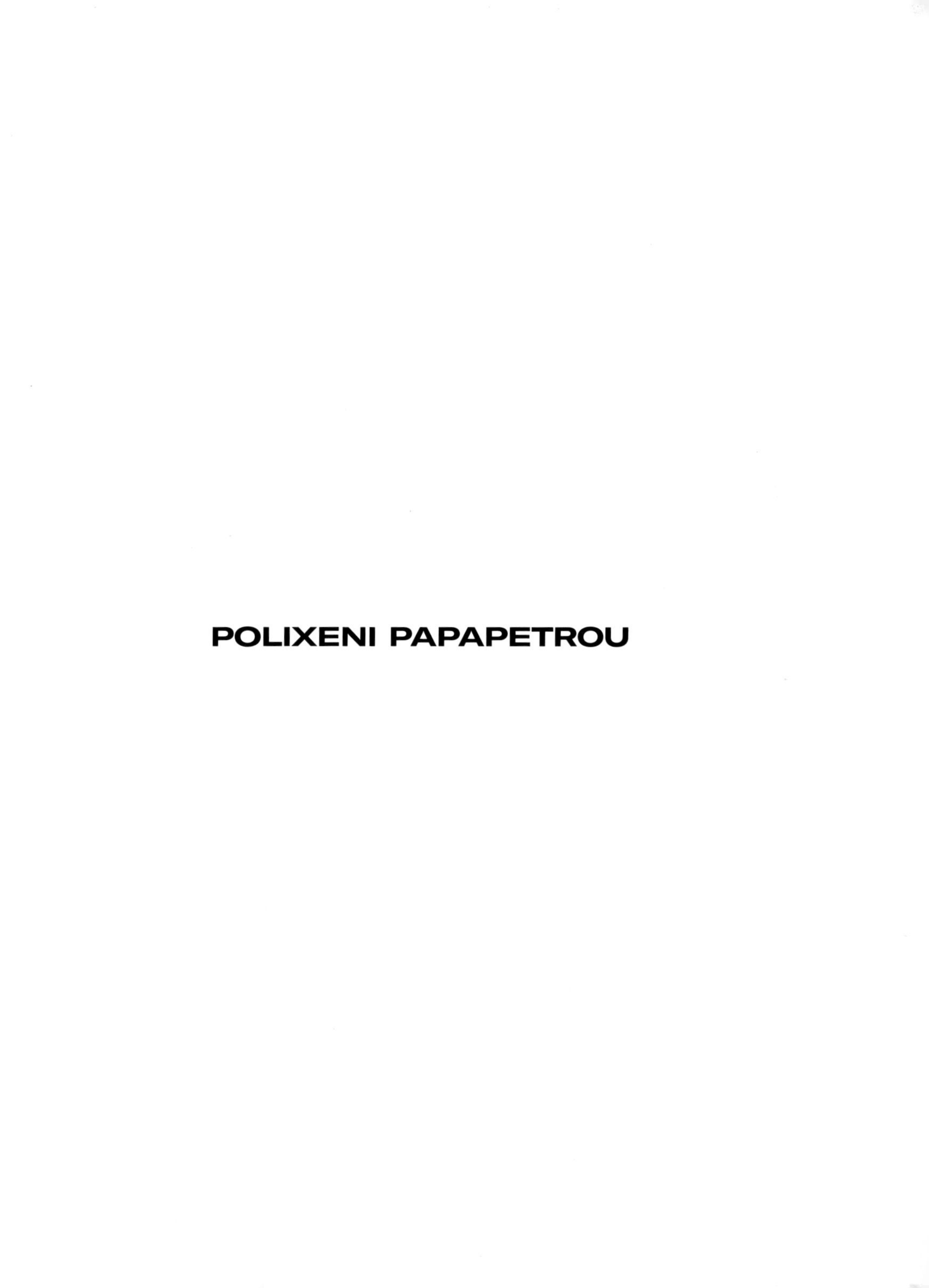

POLIXENI PAPAPETROU

POLIXENI PAPAPETROU

Series Editor Natalie King

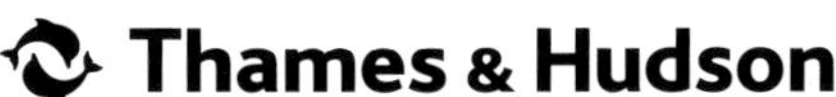

EXISTENT

ALISM AND GOOD UNDERWEAR

JOANNA MURRAY-SMITH

Polixeni Papapetrou was my kind of woman. She always epitomised to me so many of the feminine virtues – beauty, sacrifice, empathy, nurture – but always leavened by an iconoclastic wit. She was a constantly beaming lighthouse of irony, laughter and, occasionally, vulgarity. Detailed in her observations of people, not just of images, she could cite a single idiosyncratic trait that perfectly summoned a complete character. A playwright can admire this, since we are always trying to tell complex human stories quickly.

The most unusual aspect of Poli the woman was this position of observation. She managed to view things with an objective eye but was quick to forgive. There was something very moving about this, an effortless comprehension that we are all flawed, and that it is the flaws that give life drama, humour and tenderness. Perhaps that is why she was such a gracious patient, enduring the humiliations of the medical world with a robust refusal to be dimmed, as if to say: This is life, this endless shift between control and lack of control, the effort to compose ourselves and our vulnerability to decomposition, tragedy and comedy, indignity and pride.

We shared an equal pleasure in discussing profound aspects of experience: the joys and mysteries of our children, the complexities of relationships, the flaws in friendships, and our love–hate affairs with our own work – and much more ordinary fare. We gave equal time to existentialism and good underwear. We could move conversationally from how we are all bound to our mothers for good and ill to what Nicole Kidman wore at the Emmys. Poli travelled deeply and lightly all at once, skimmed the surface and redefined the deepest depths for me. Her mind presented an ever-evolving kaleidoscope of life: emotion, celebrity, struggle, epiphany, style, mortality. These themes were part of our conversation and the architecture of Poli's professional storytelling.

The two most enchanting and baffling aspects of her life's productivity are her children and her photography. No amount of declared innovation can quite camouflage that we are captivated by certain stories which begin in the ramshackle reaches of our childhood. As young creators, we may think that creative drive is always taking us into new domains. As older artists, we are forced to see that new territory is usually a reimagining of old territory. It takes an emotionally mature artist to not be threatened by their own repetition but embrace it. I always saw in Poli a fellow-traveller in how, as artists, we are at the mercy of the unconscious and how our recurring preoccupations are evidence of this.

The older I become, the more I realise that the obsessions and proclivities an artist returns to over and over are drawn from the well of early experience. We return to them because they hold us hostage and creative maturity is more about surrender than resistance. We give ourselves over to the unconscious because we instinctively understand the futility.

When I look at Poli's work, I see the flourishing that came from that acceptance. In these pages, seeing the work in 'Sensurround' – across youth, love, study, work, parenting and illness – allows us to see those psychological commandments that draw a thread through time and the body of a life's work.

When Poli's own children, Olympia and Solomon, took the space that Elvis fans and impersonators, drag queens, wrestlers and bodybuilders had once filled, I was seduced. Her eye shifted to the intricacies of her own small drama, as her heart did. Children are never just children in Poli's work. They are in a tug of war between themselves and the world around them. The carefully curated props hurl them into other contexts and characters, camouflaging their own secret intent. I have always seen myself in those images, as I'm sure others do. They summon my own conflicted sense of identity in the netherworld of pre-teen and teen – when I was part servant to the adult world, part superior to it. I think I knew that children may be at the mercy of adult whims, but they have what adults can never have again and that collapse between vulnerability and power is buried deep in Poli's imagery.

The turn towards childhood would not surprise any artist–mother, since the experience of birth and child-raising creates its own volatile, captivating world. Watching a human come into itself turns the artist–mother into a whimsical Joseph Banks, recording the specific, wondrous and intimate details of these new discoveries as if they had never been seen before. After years of looking out at the world, the world that is closest to you becomes rife with possibility, enlarged by emotion. I see Poli's ego in her images of her children, who reflect her power and narcissism, as they do in all mothers' creative work – but they also add a kind of humility to her images. Despite our best intentions, our children will become themselves. The how of that is the story of the artist–mother's evolution.

Poli brilliantly engaged and captured the terrifying savoir faire of children, as well as their beauty, the playground of identity and camouflage and embellishment, and a child's effortless celebrity (especially when they are our own). The techniques and contexts change, but each photographic chapter is part of a continuum that evolves in more and more interesting ways.

I witnessed how time manifested through Poli's eye. She graciously accepted the borders around her creative playing field and played so inventively within it. Filled with sky and sand and bush and flora, her subjects play between the real world and artifice, between actual children and their transforming masks, between a painted landscape and a natural one, between childhood's uncontrollable urges and the controlling nature of the camera which holds still – for a split second – its urgent forward momentum.

Whenever I left Poli, I drove home with a head full of interesting thoughts. Like Poli herself, her photographs ask more questions than they answer. Her work plays with ambiguities and abstractions, moral conundrums and self-awareness, because that was the terrain of her charismatic mind. Innocence collided with the sophisticated manipulations of art to provoke and excite us, just as our lively and life-enhancing conversations travelled twin roads of poetry and profanity.

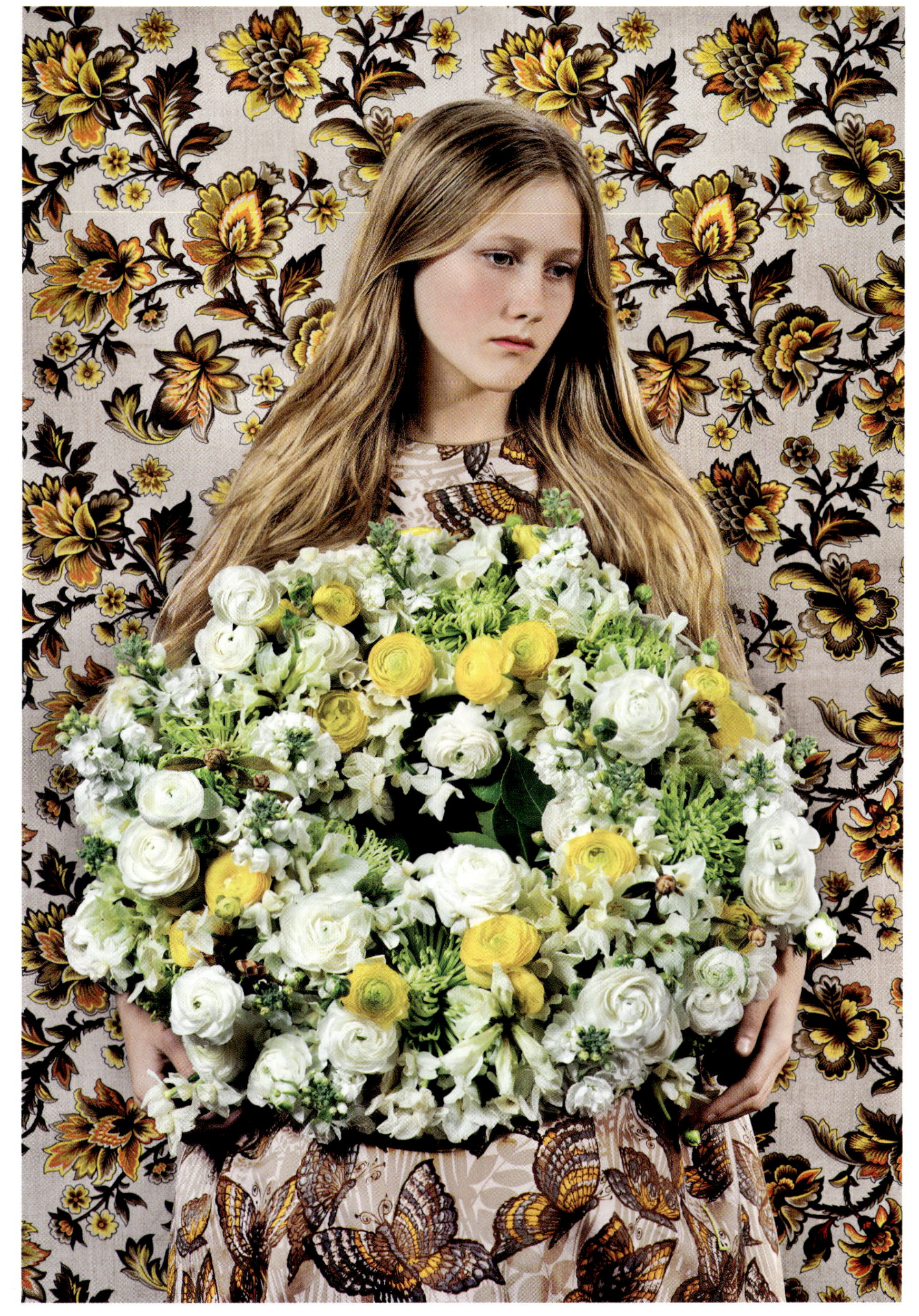

Flora
2016

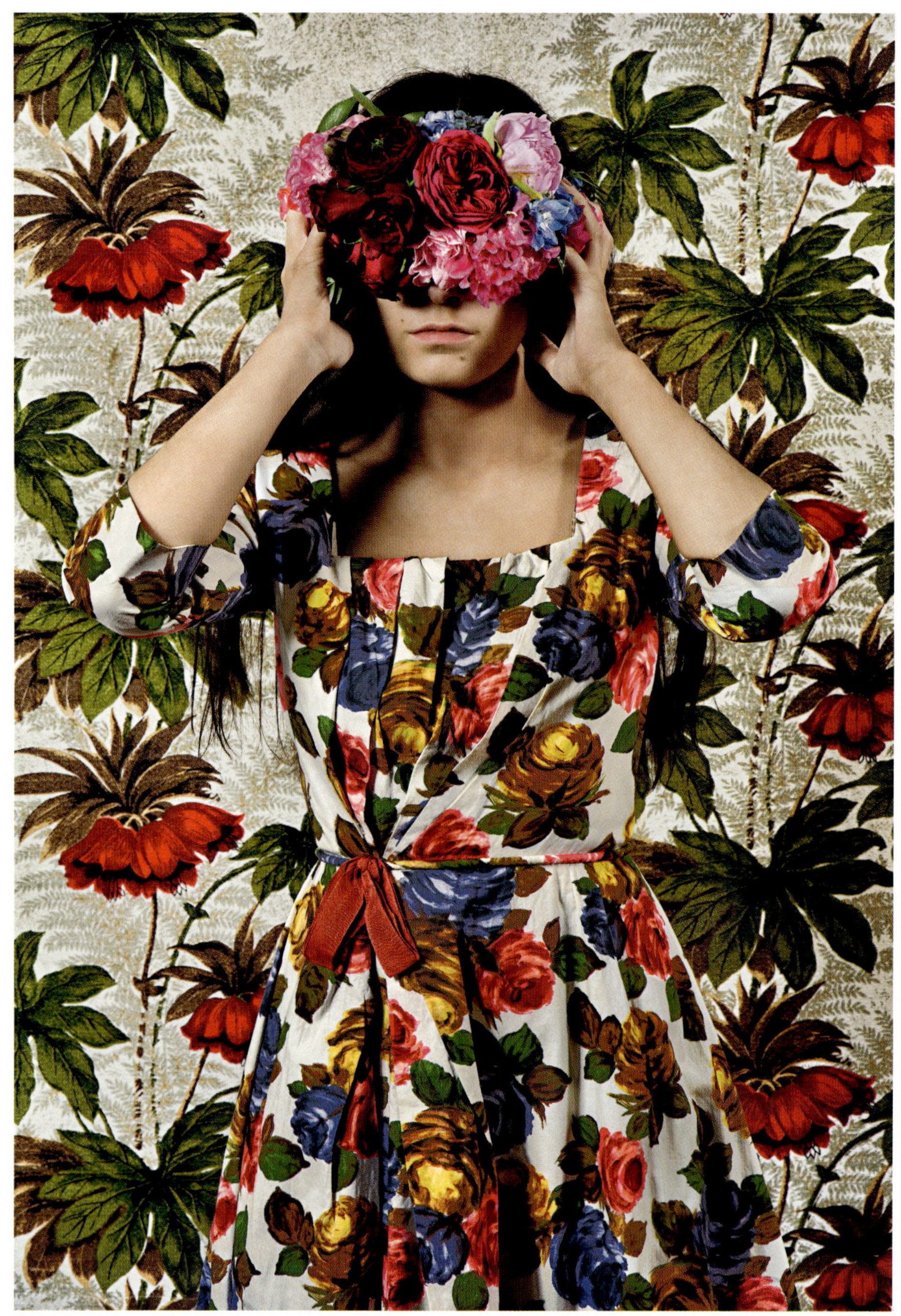

Blinded
2016

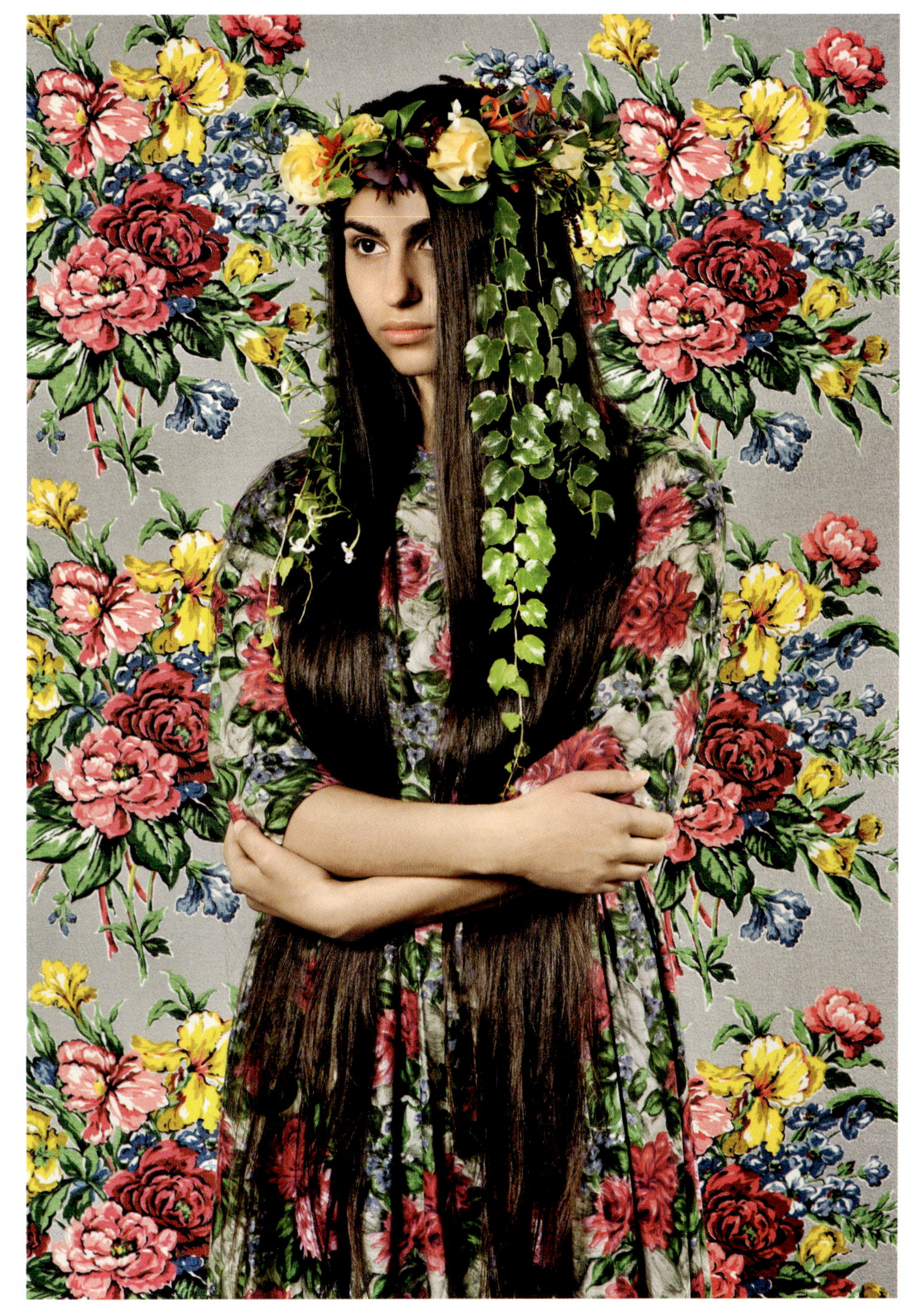

Delphi
2016

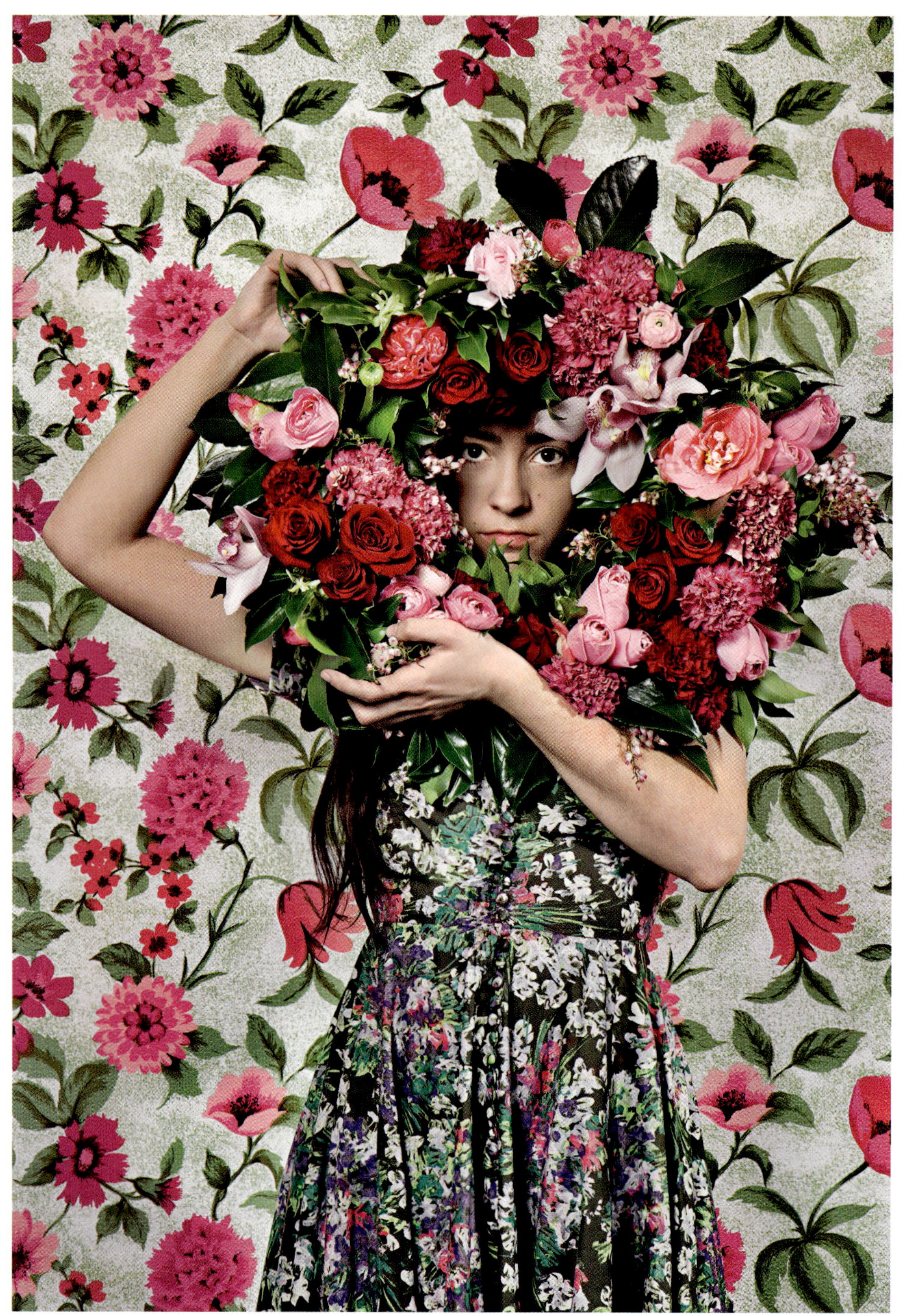

Amaranthine
2016

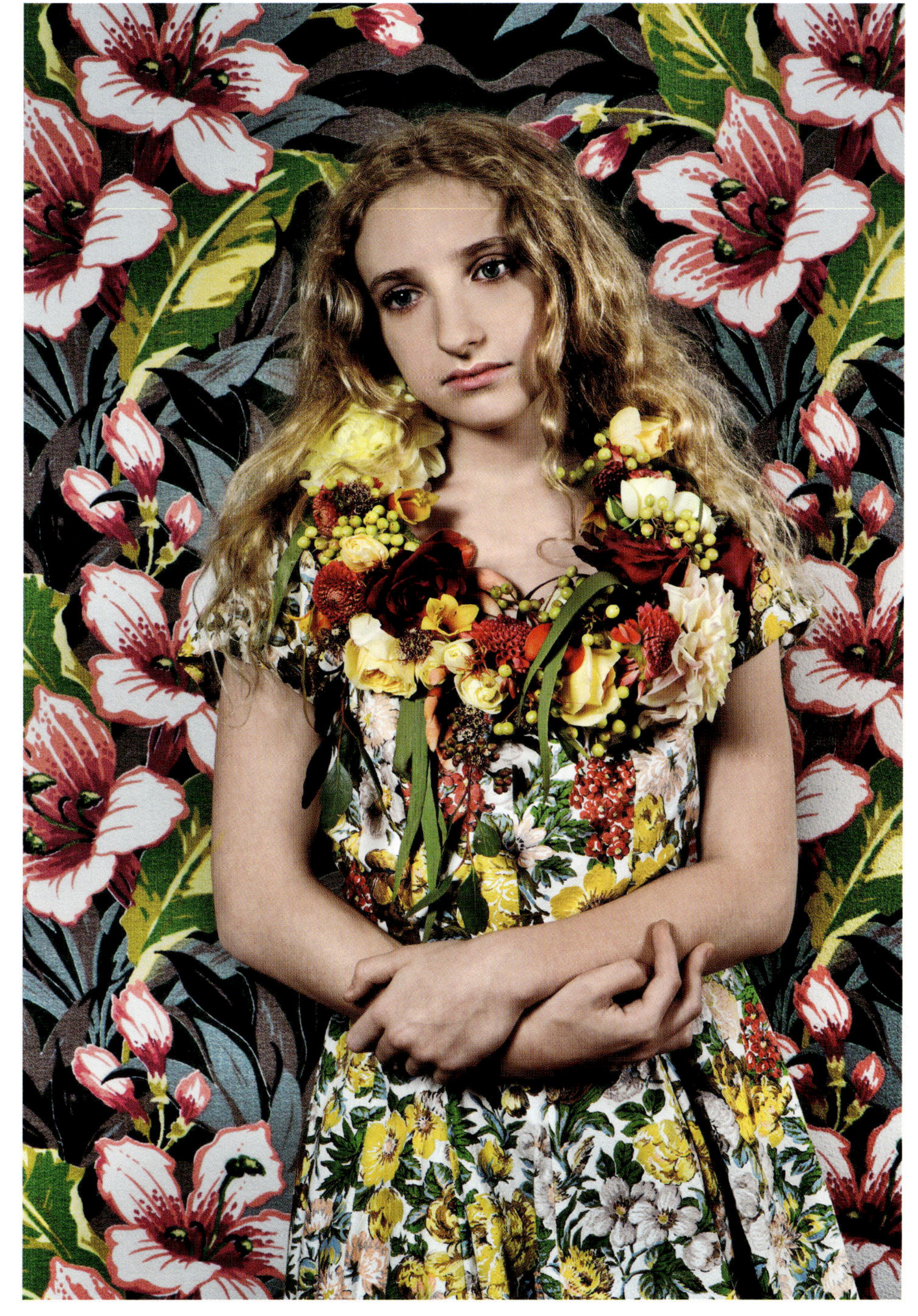

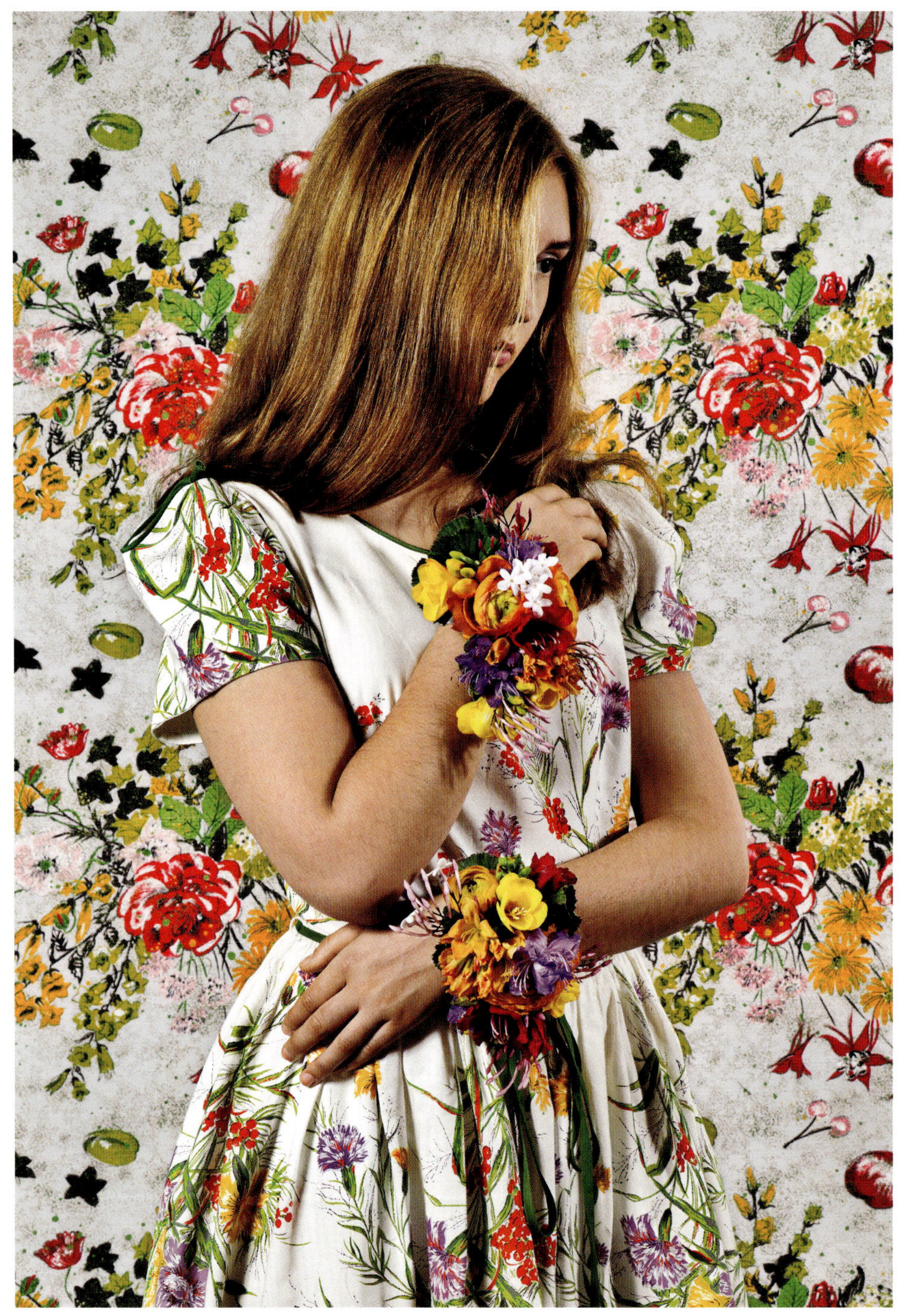

Amaryllis
2016

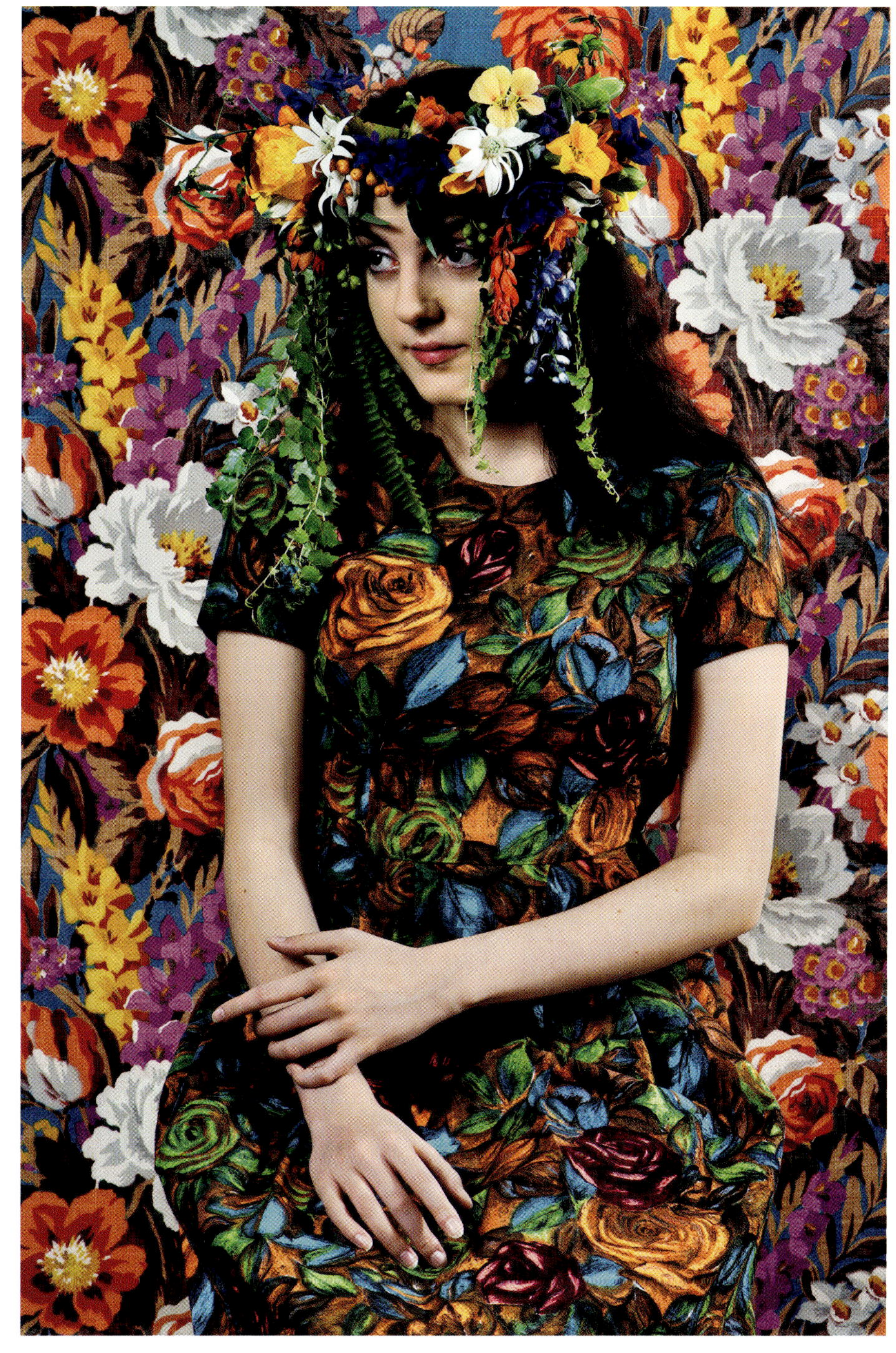

Psyche
2016

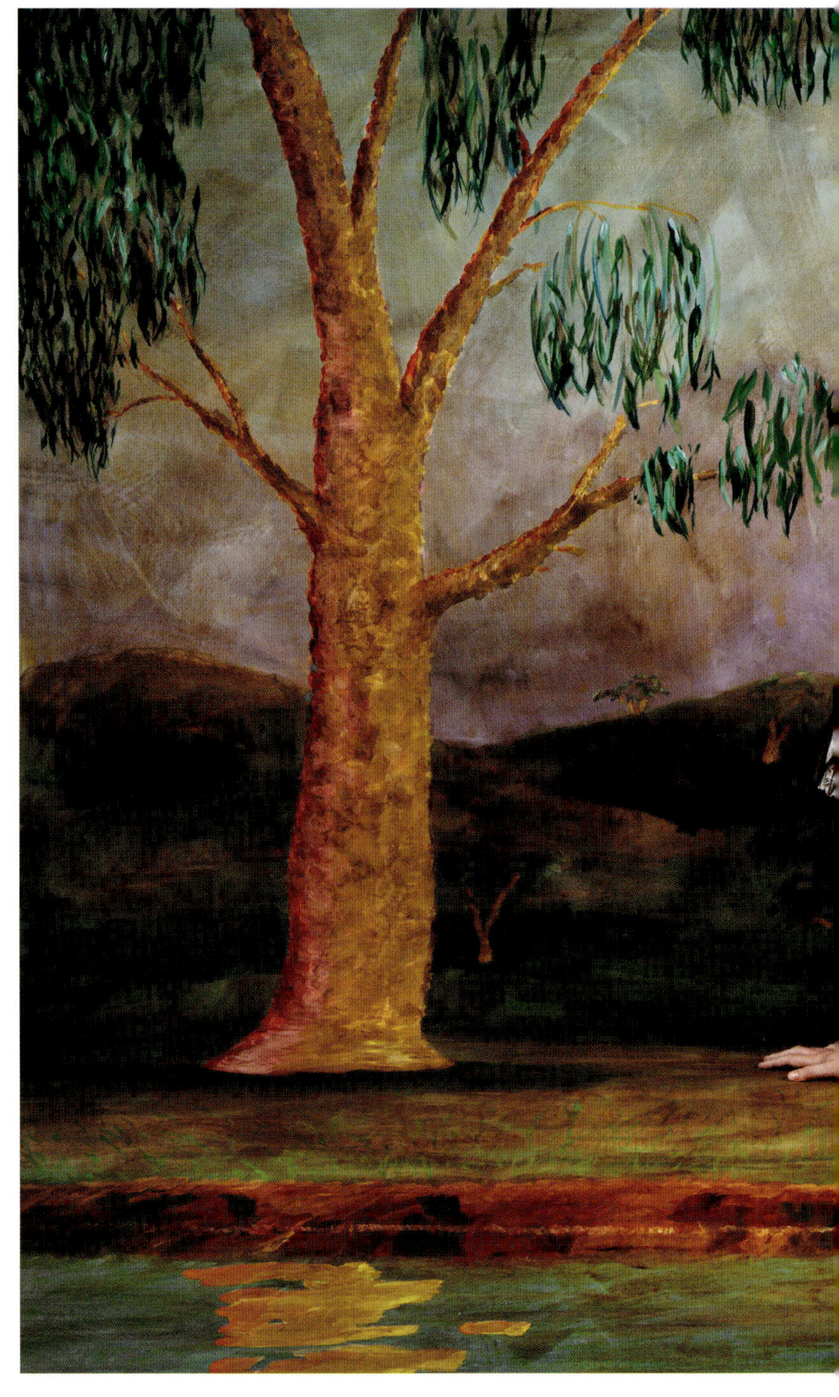

The Story Teller
2014

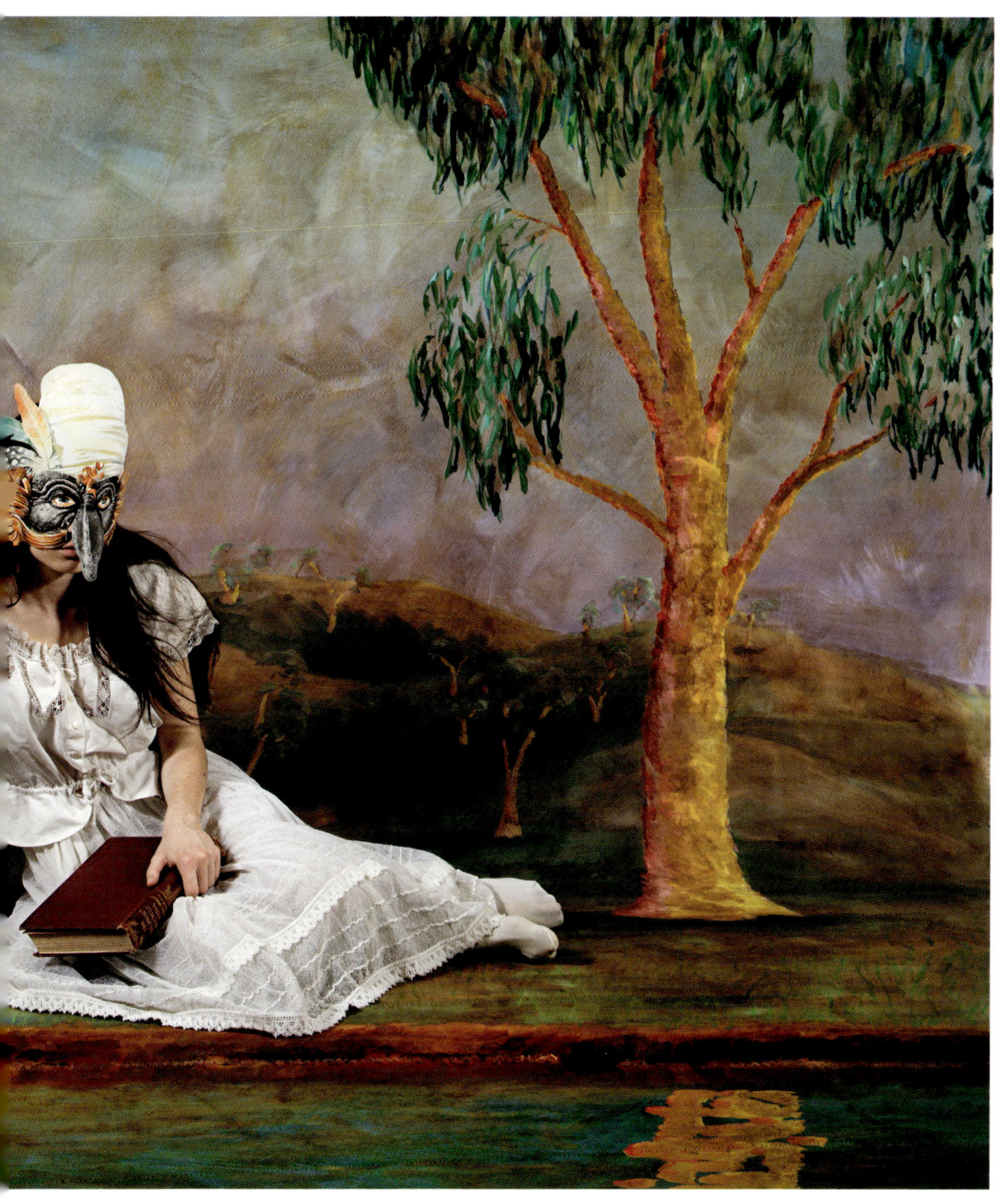

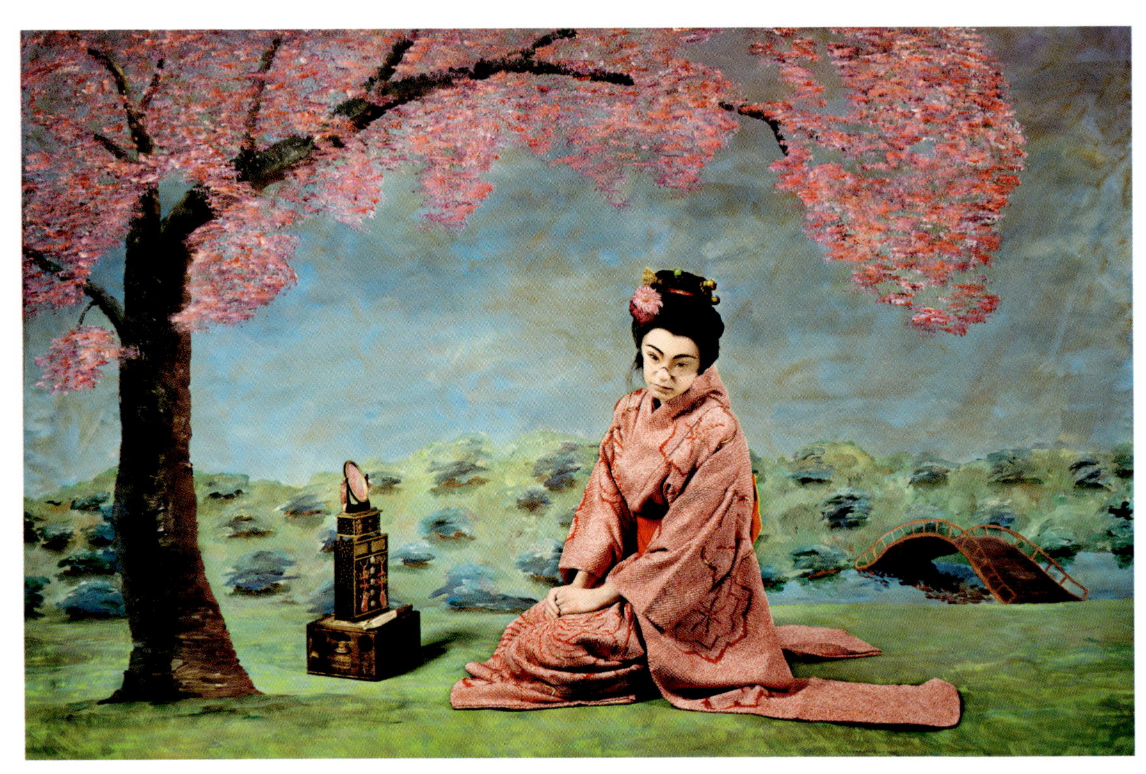

The Orientalist
2014

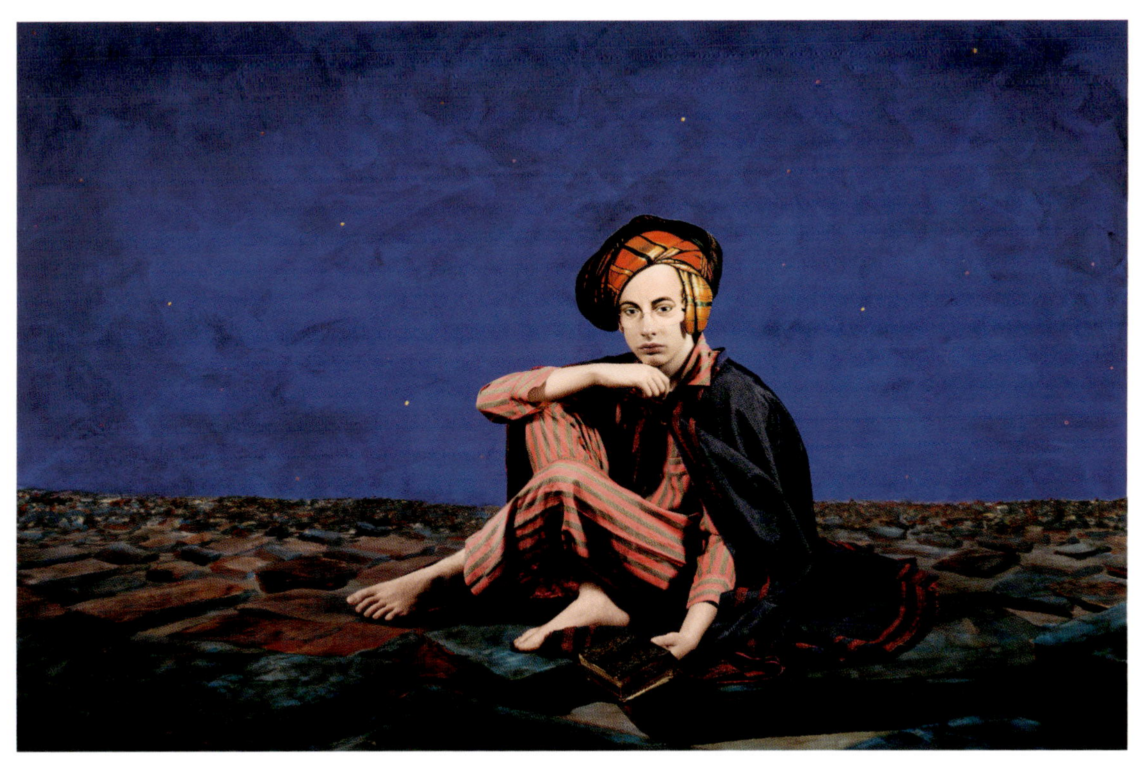

The Poet
2014

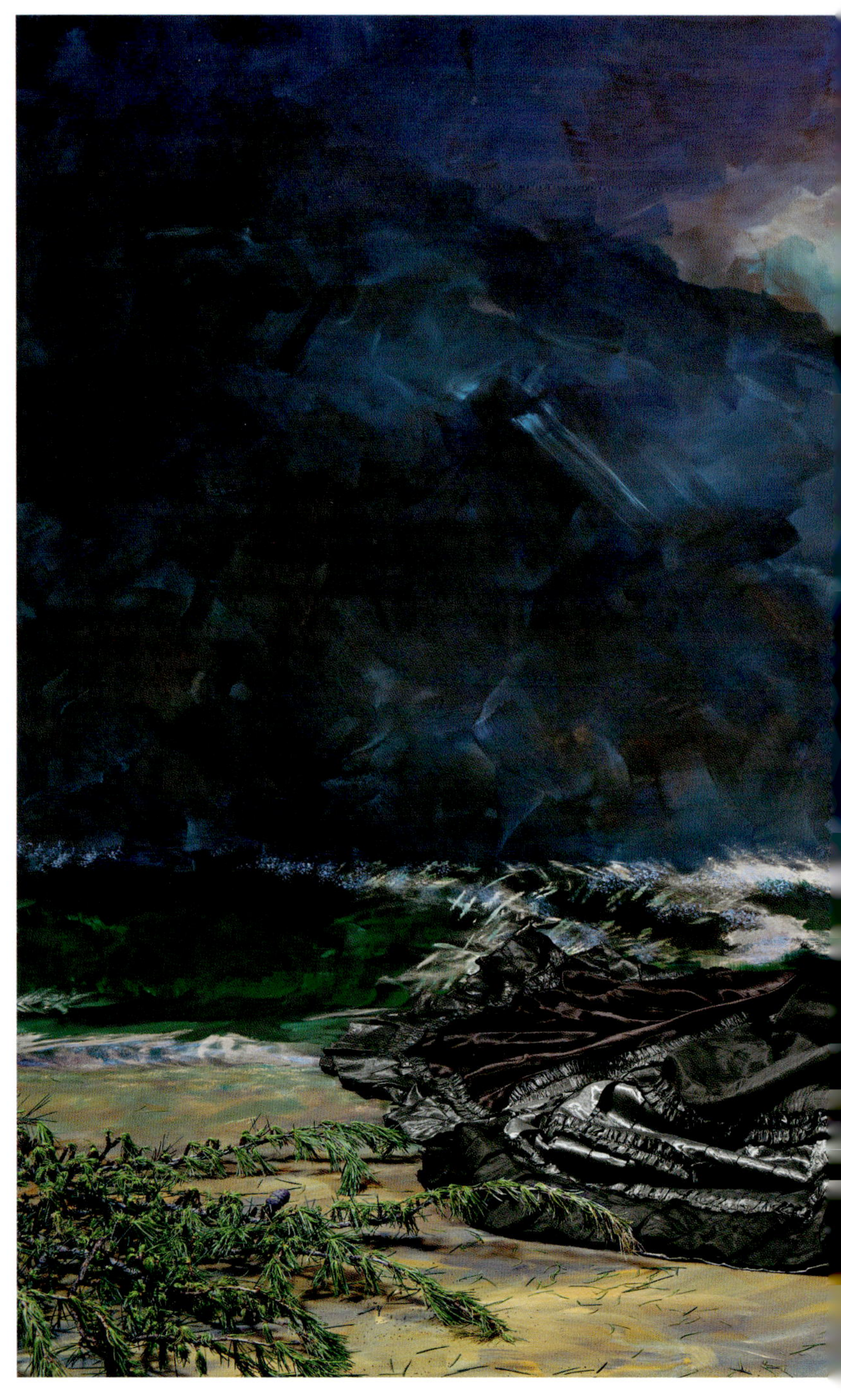

The Immigrant
2014

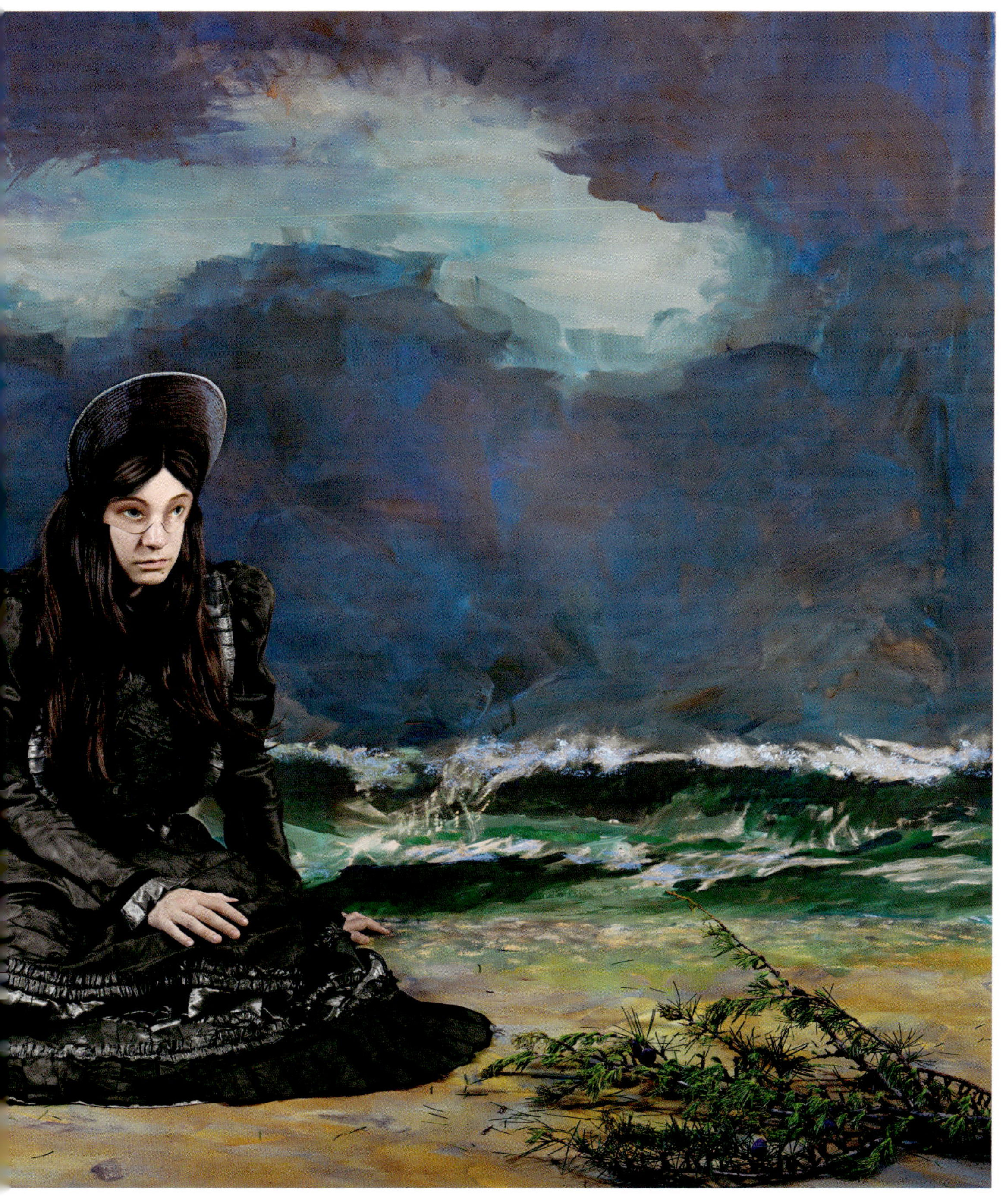

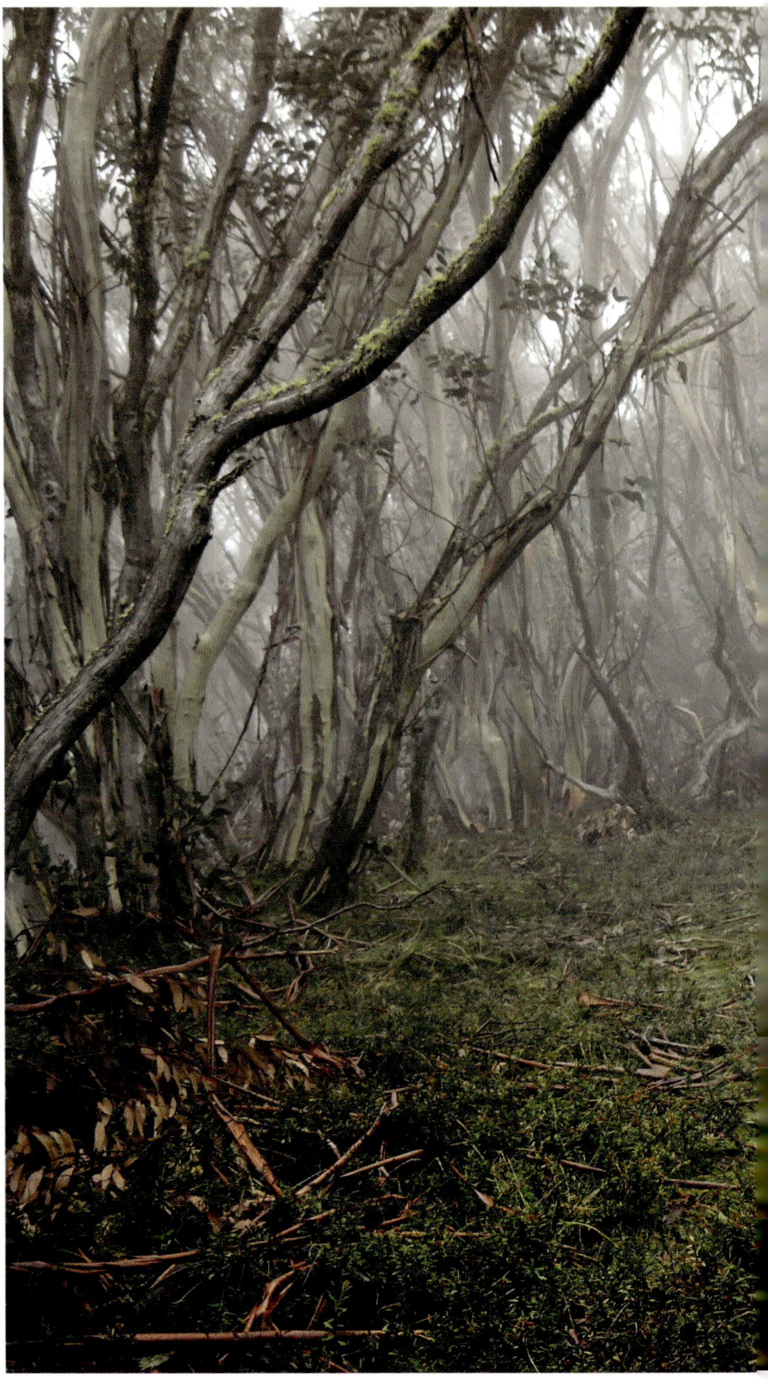

The Visitor
2012

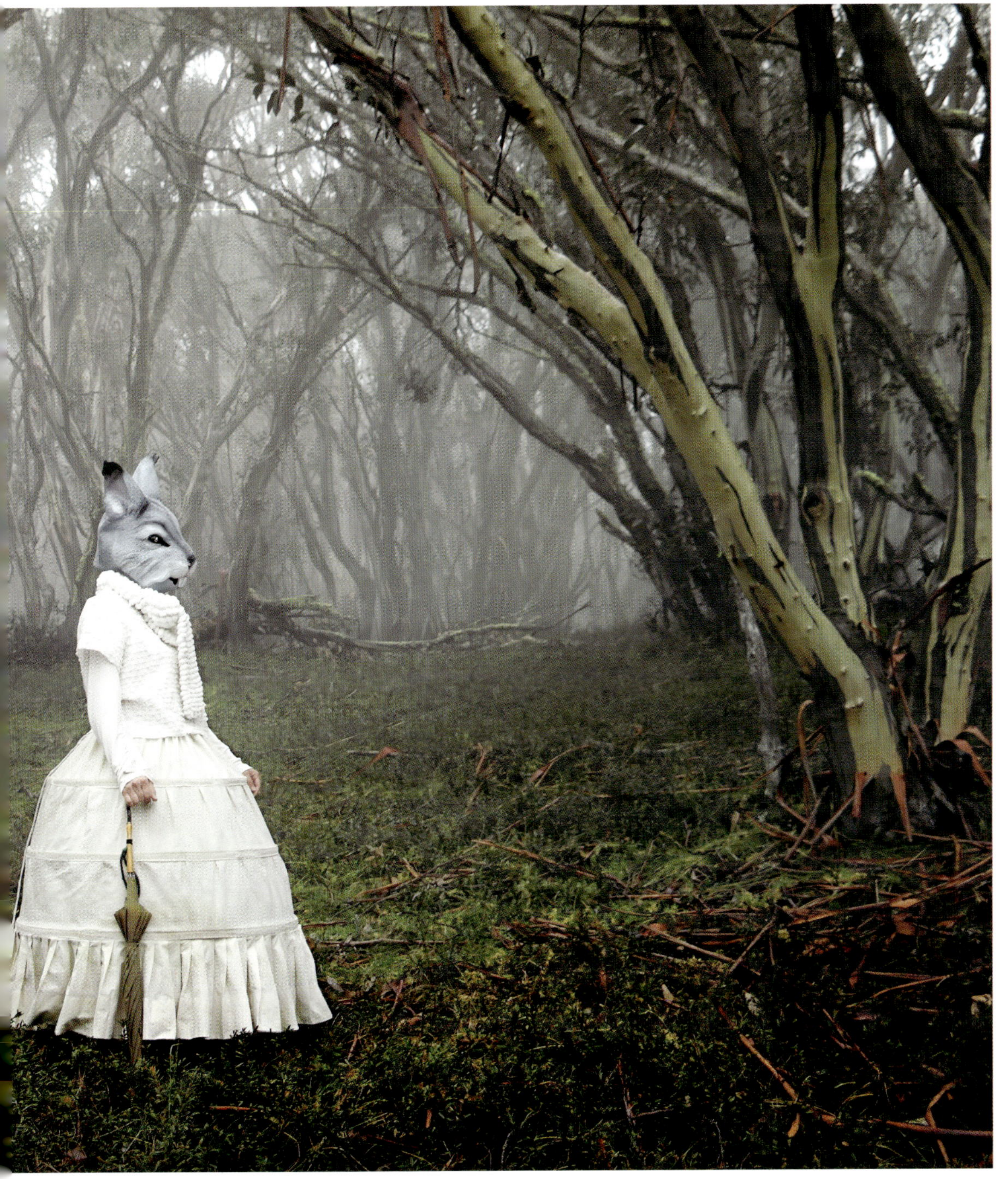

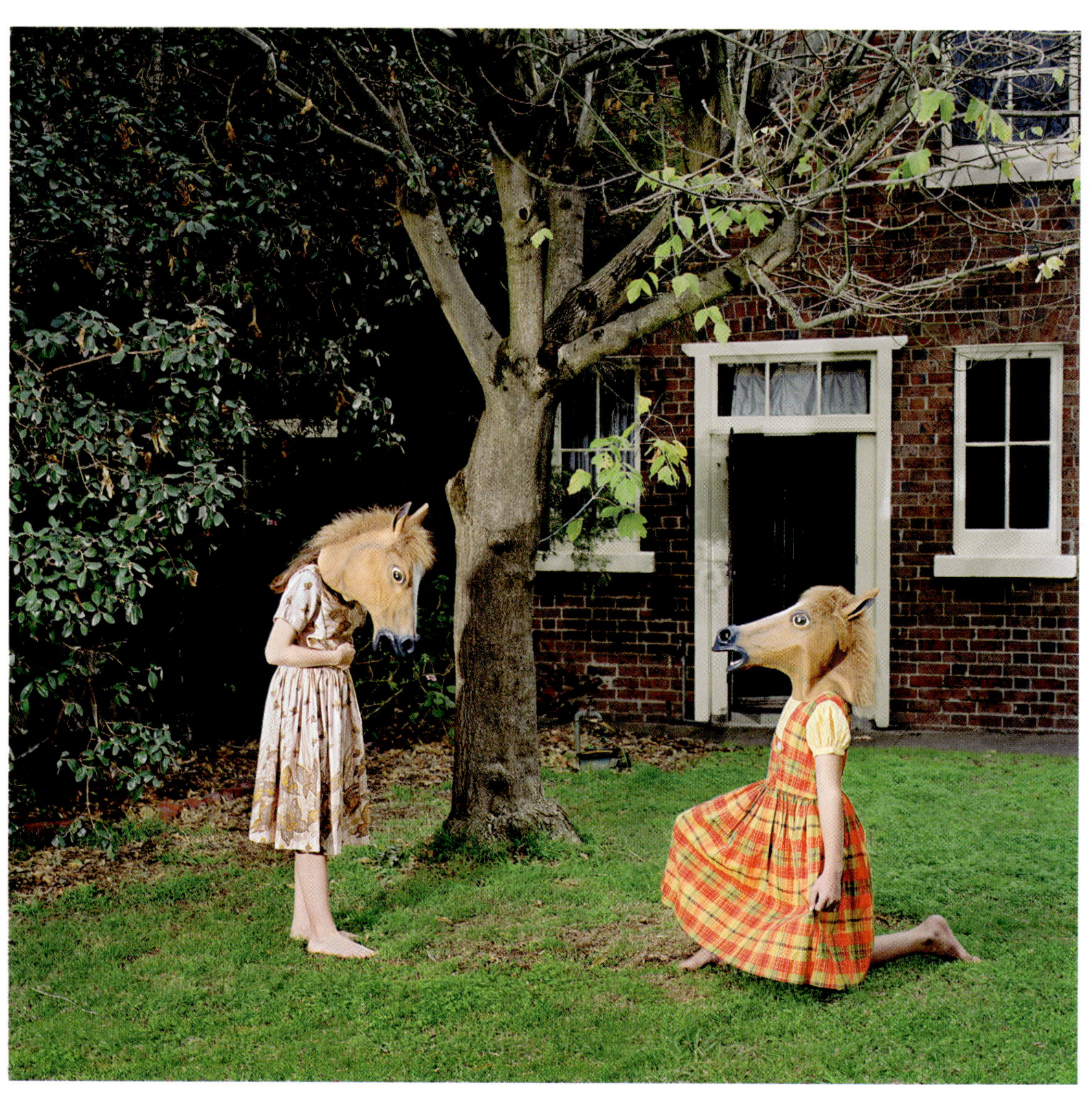

The Players
2009

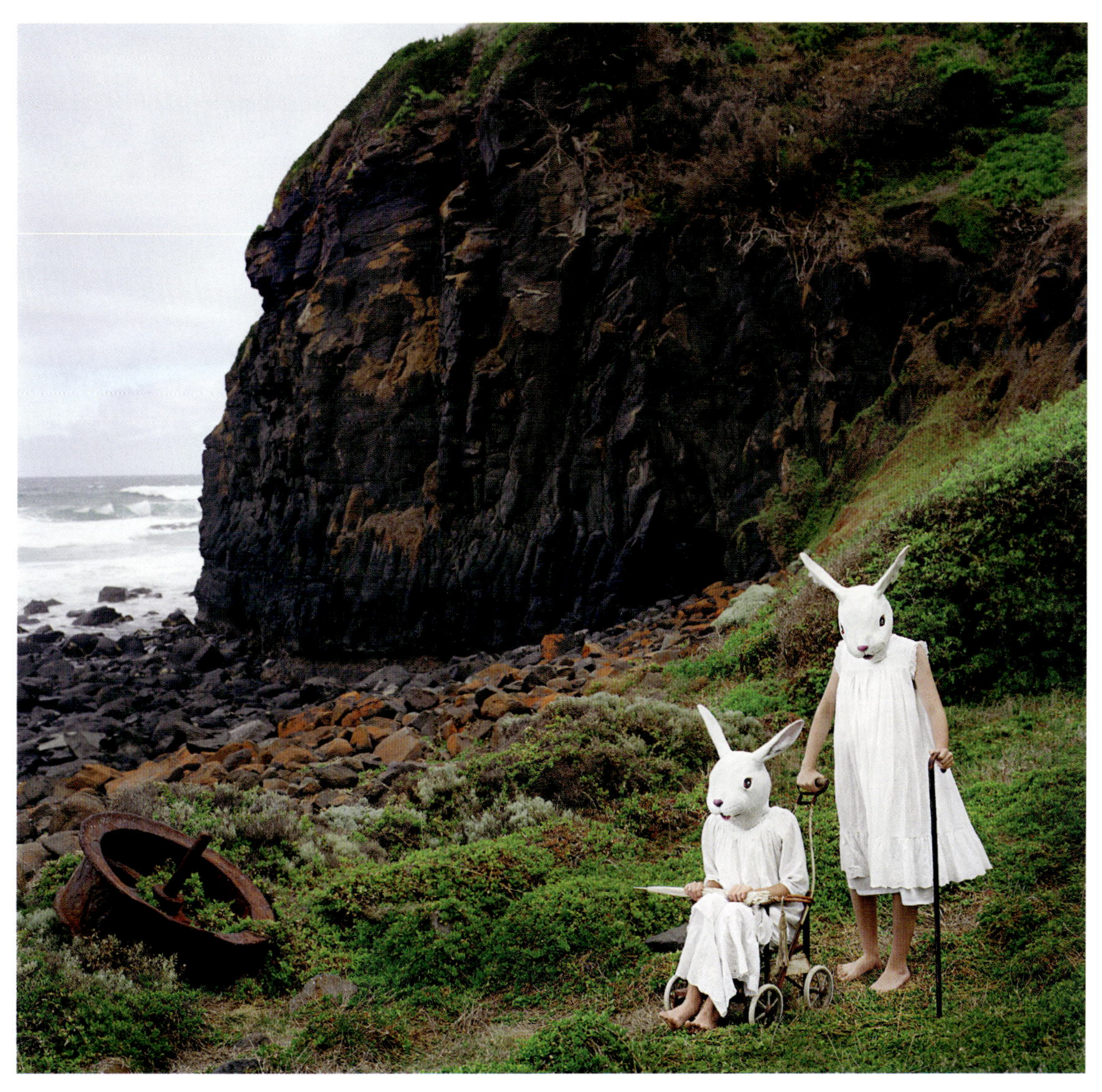

The Loners
2009

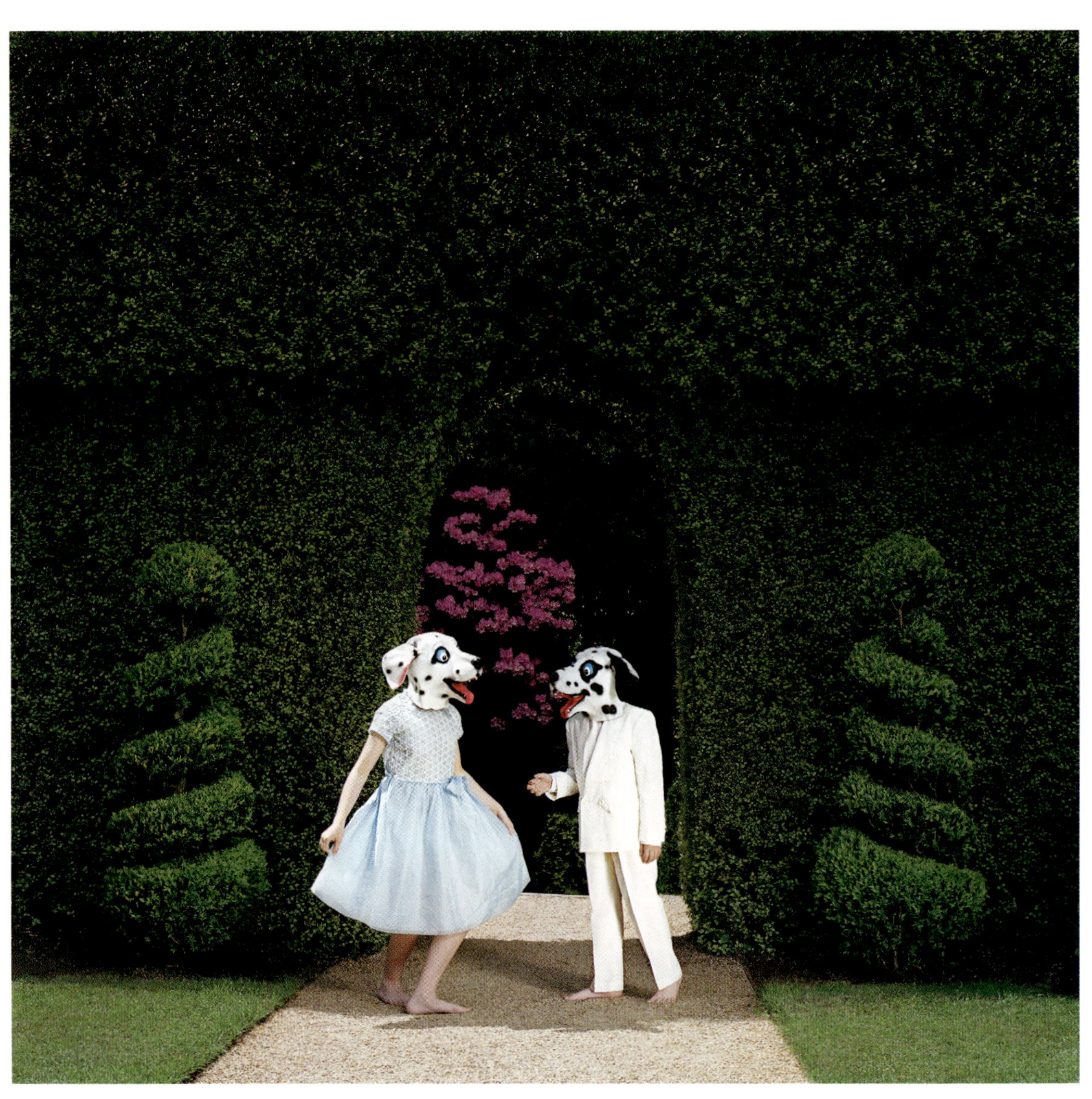

The Debutants
2009

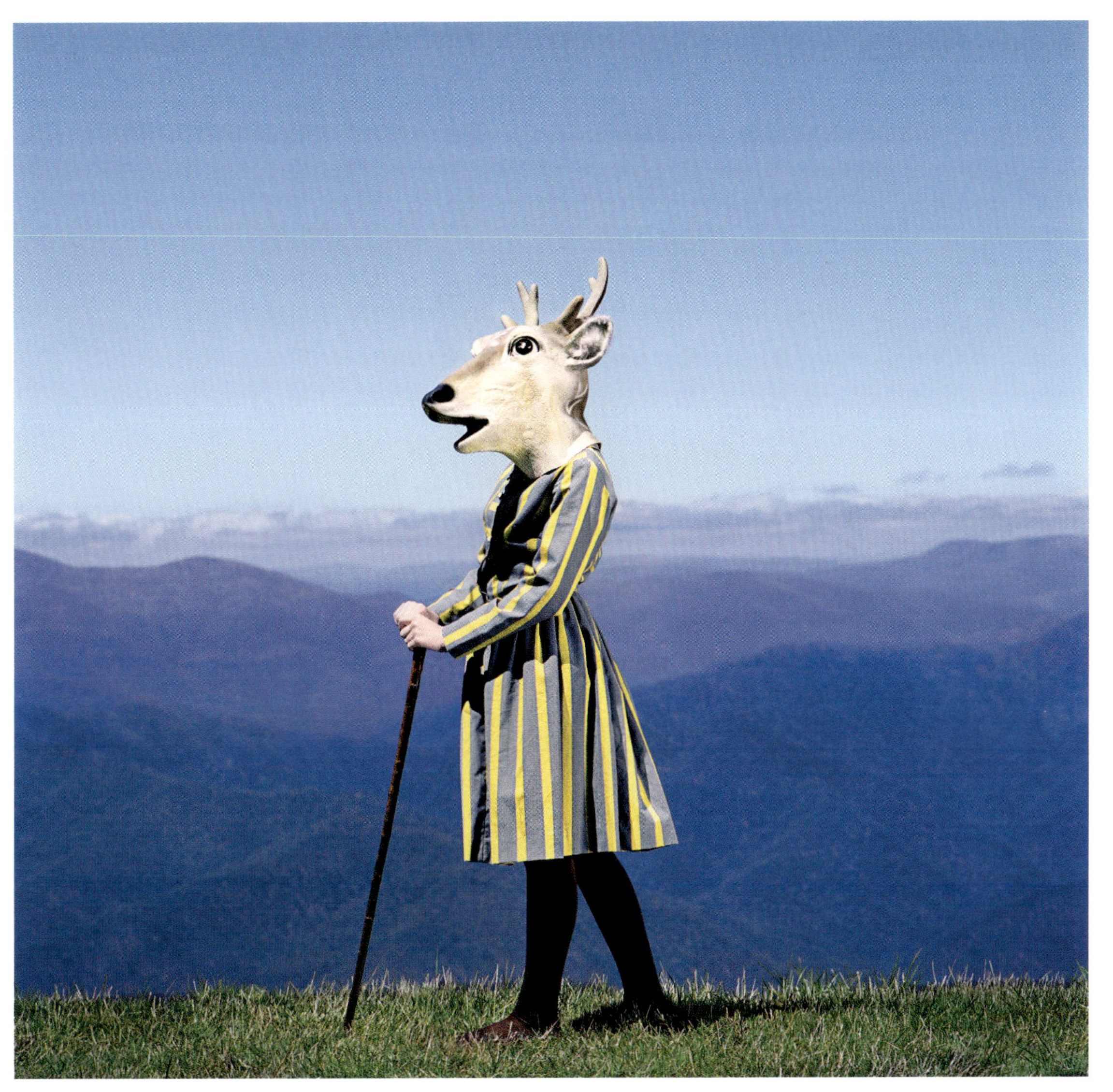

The Wanderer
2009

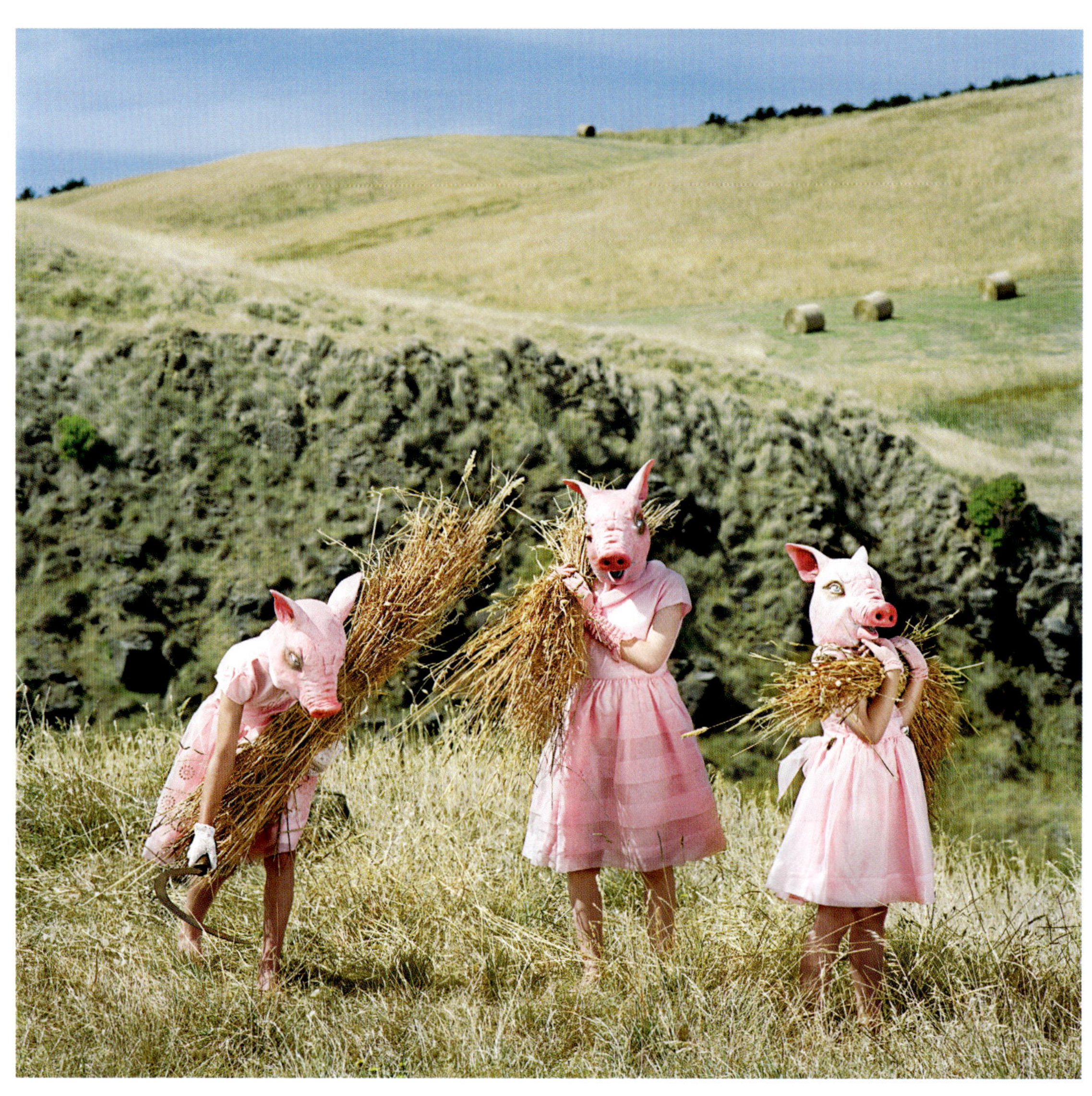

The Harvesters
2009

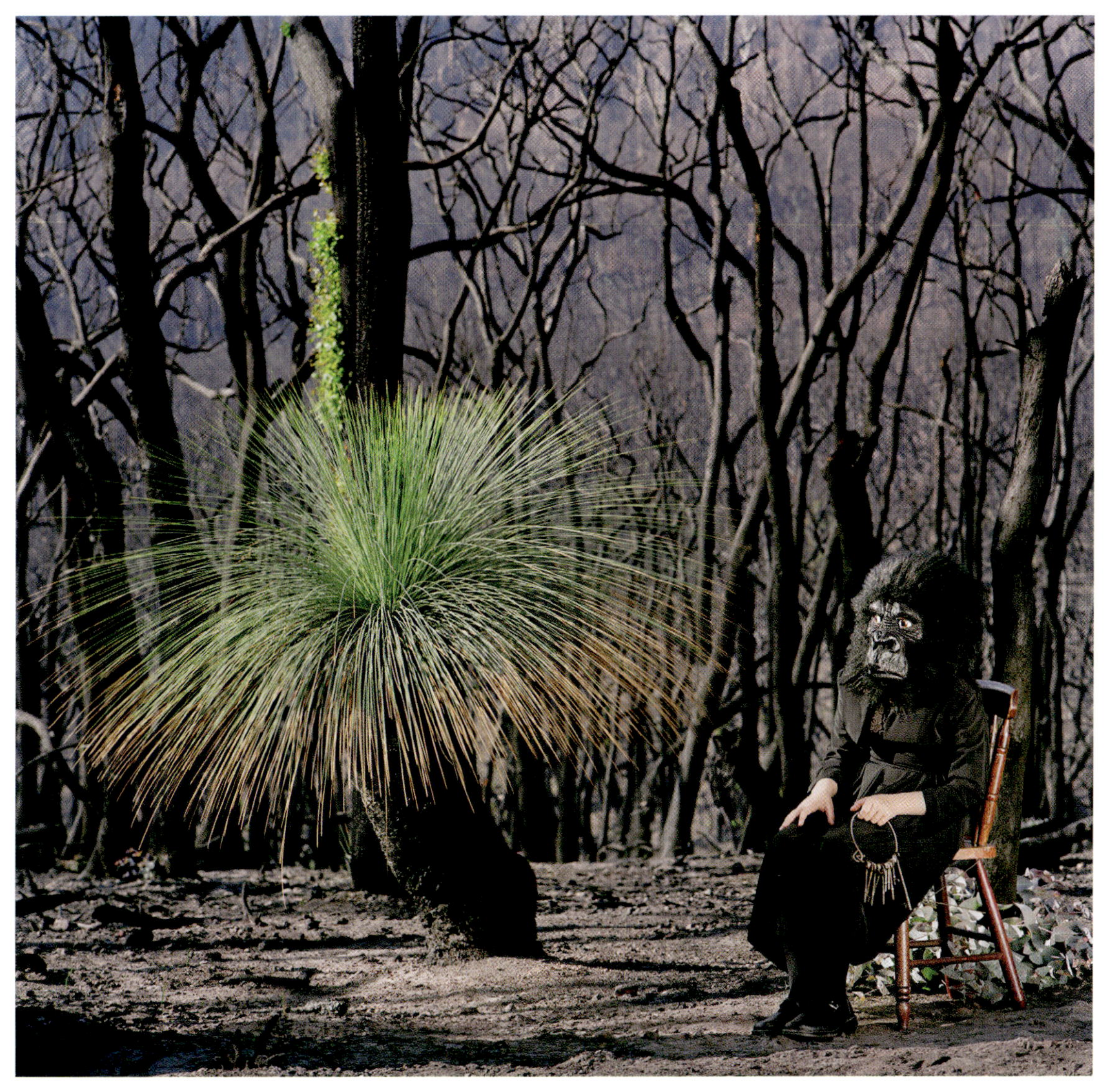

The Caretaker
2009

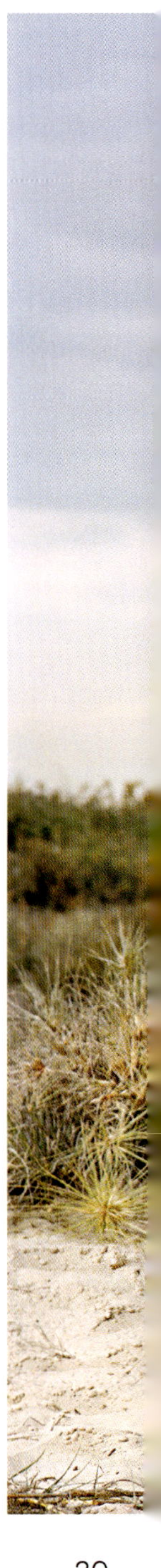

The Mourner
2012

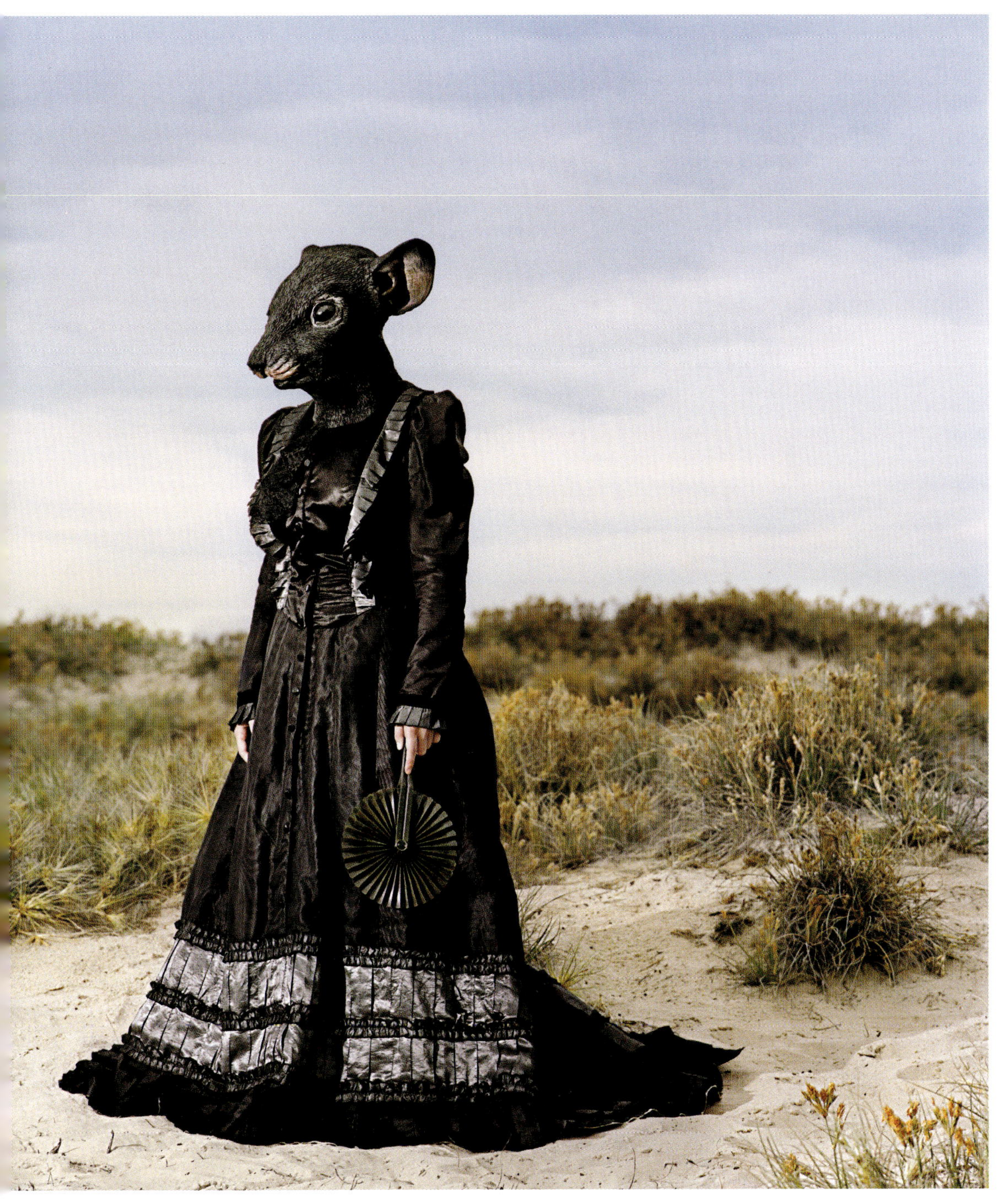

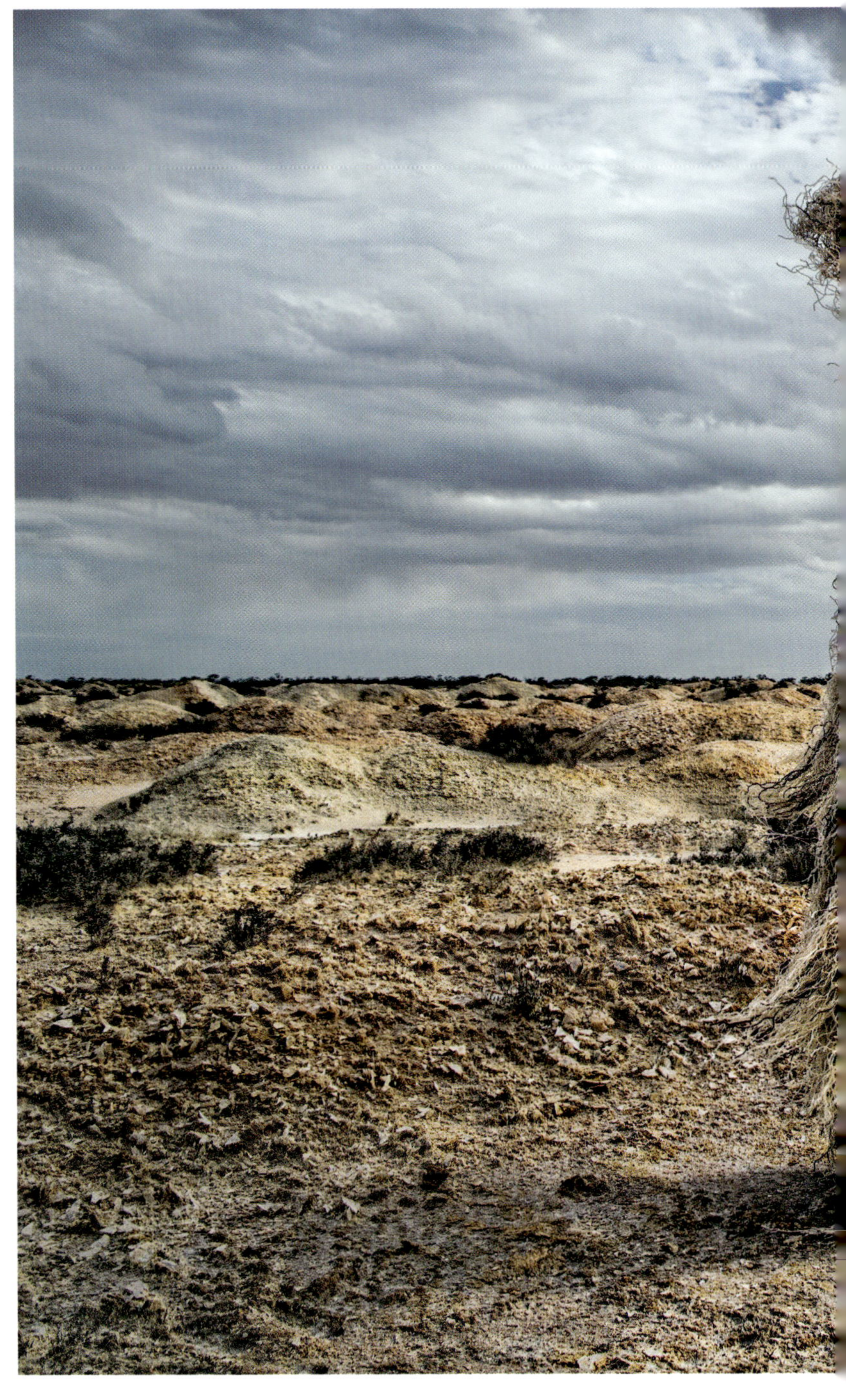

Study for Hattah Man and Hattah Woman
2013

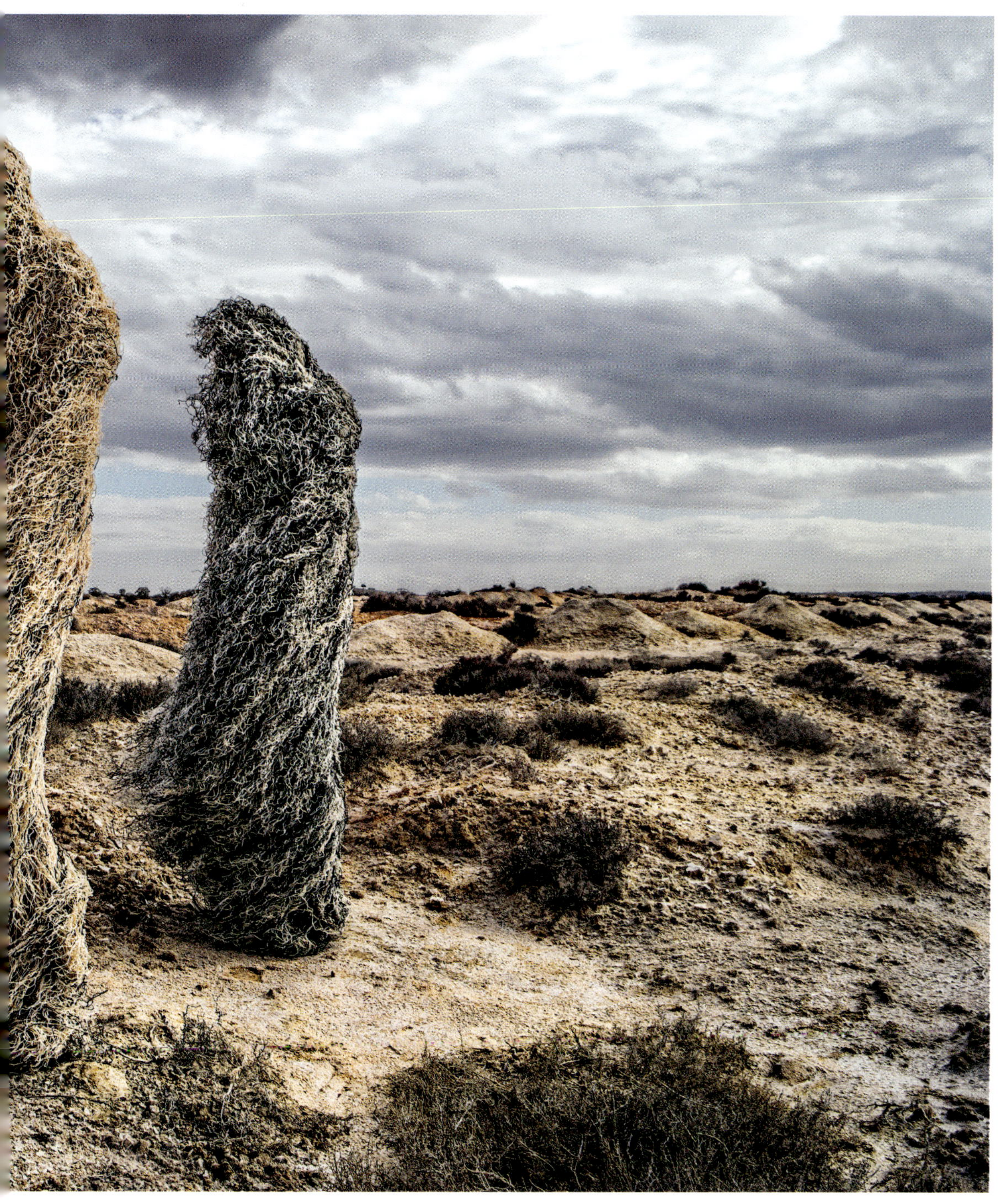

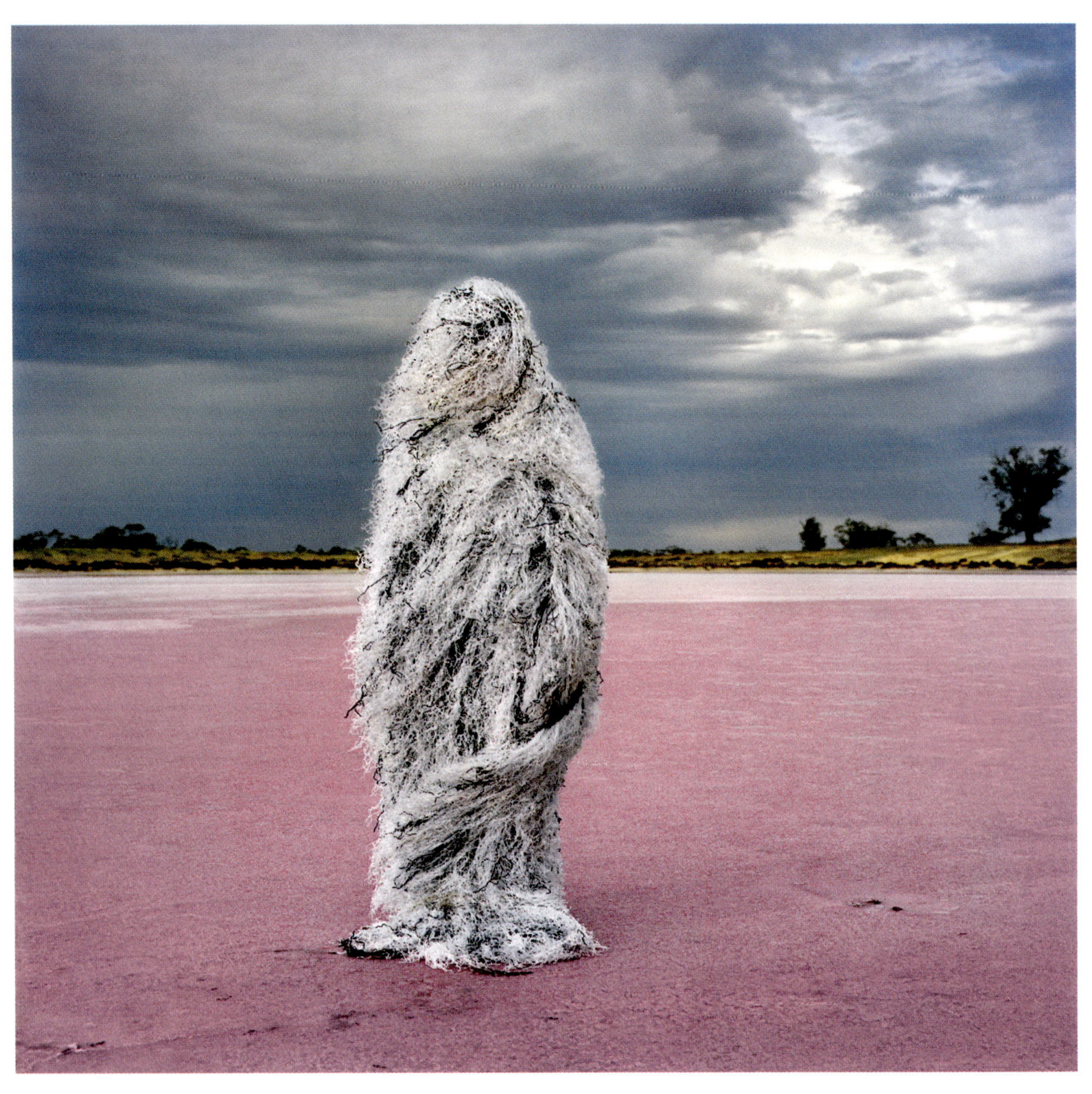

Salt Man
2013

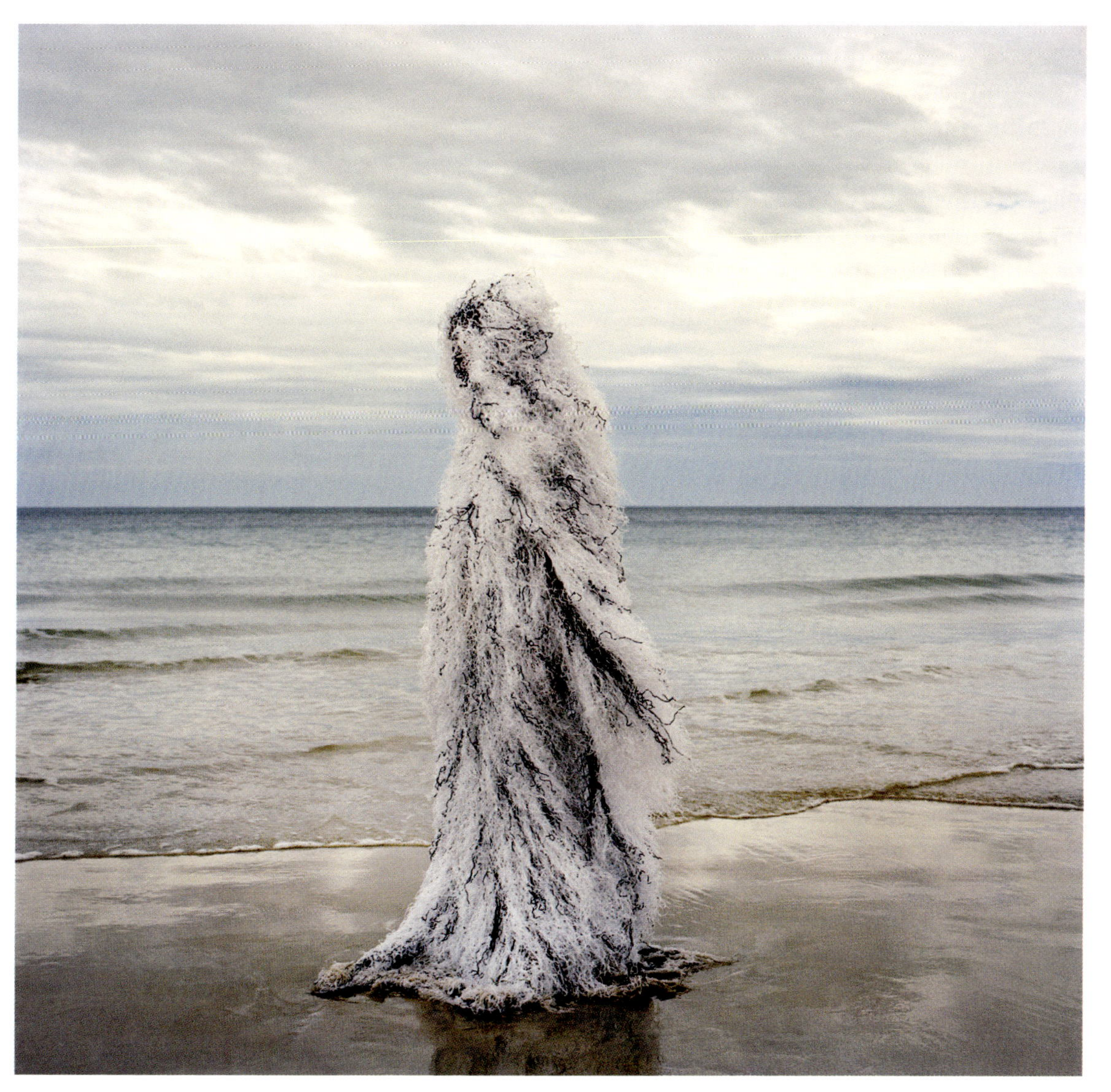

Ocean Man
2013

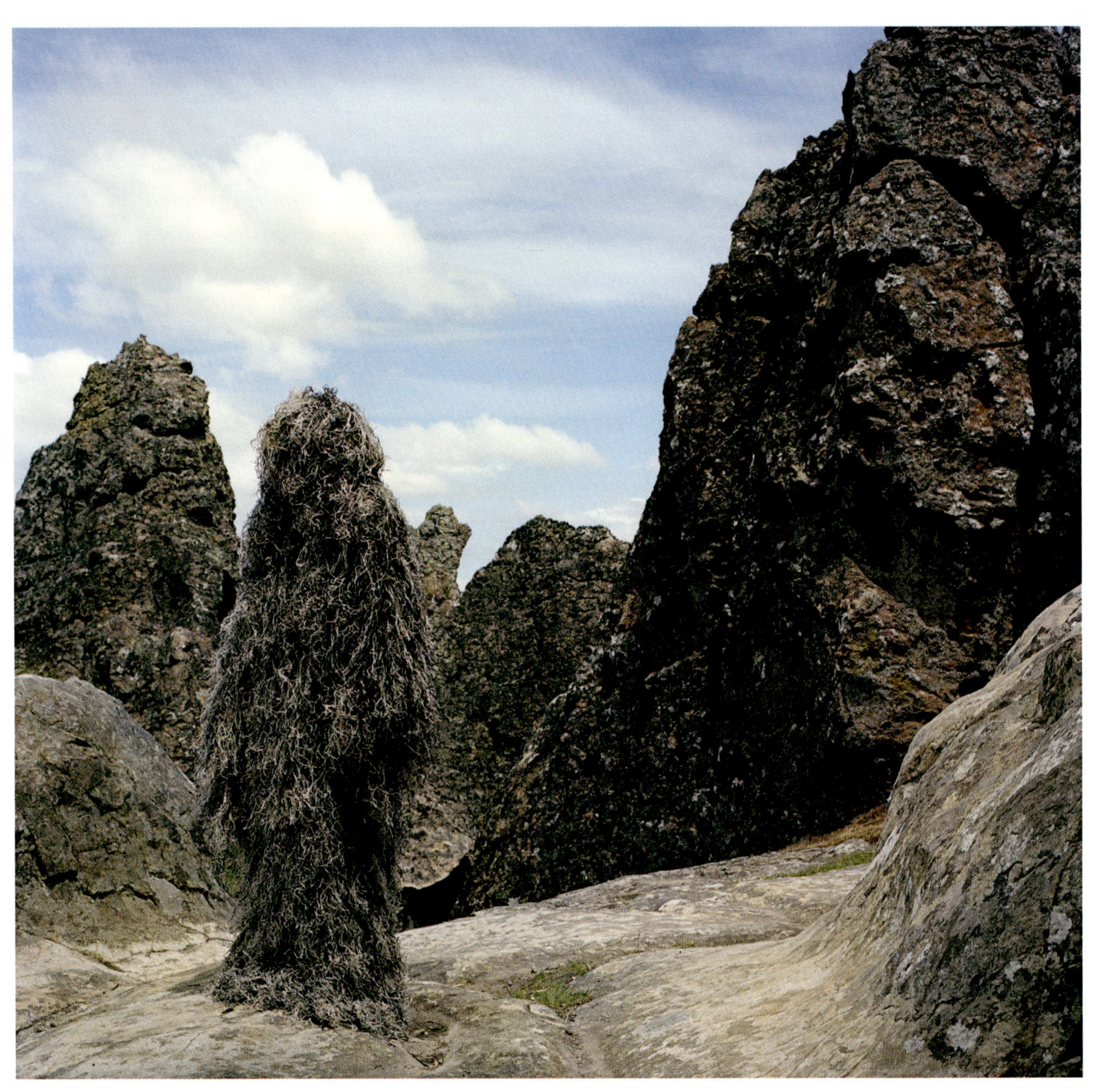

Magma Man
2013

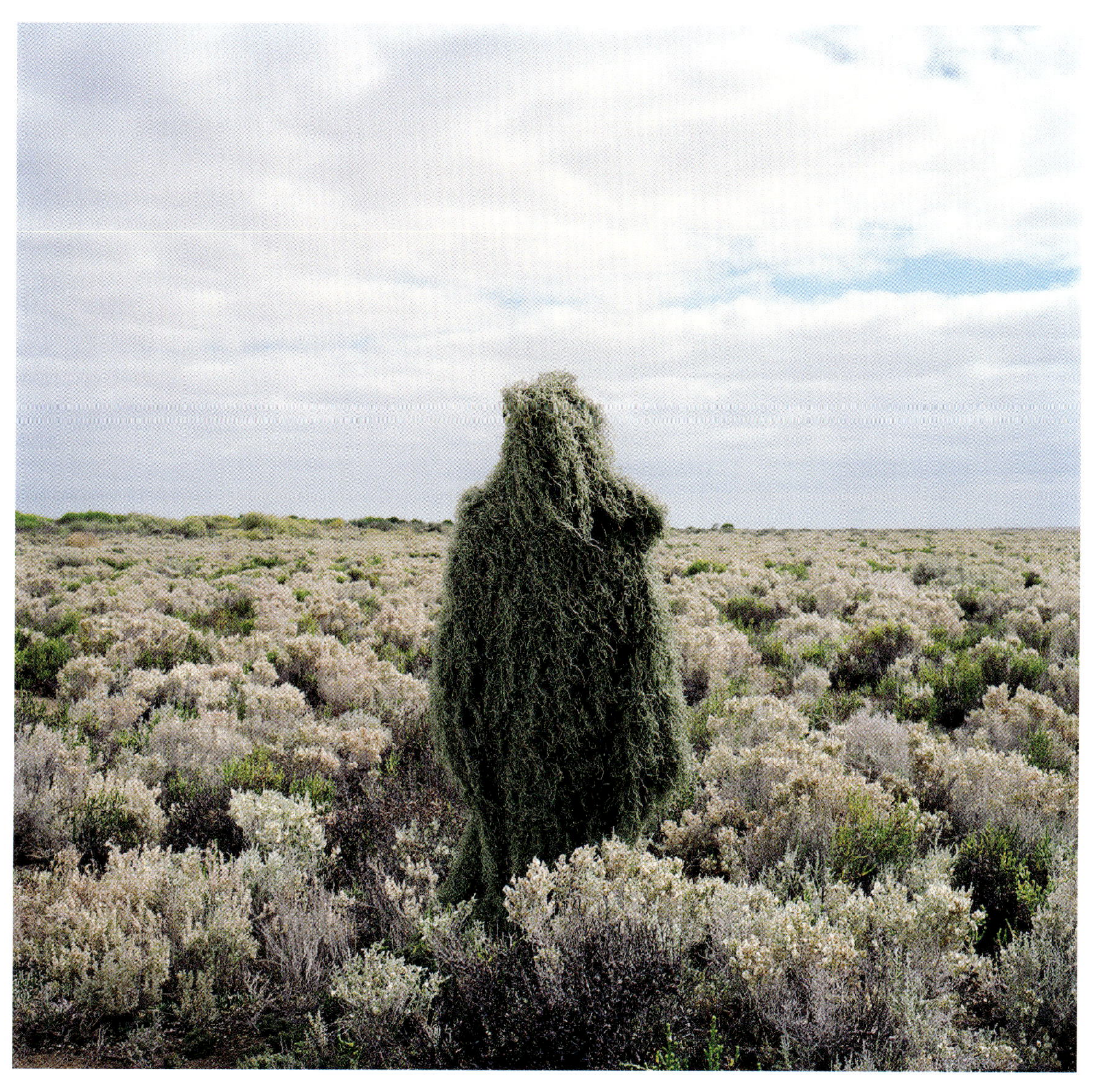

Scrub Man
2013

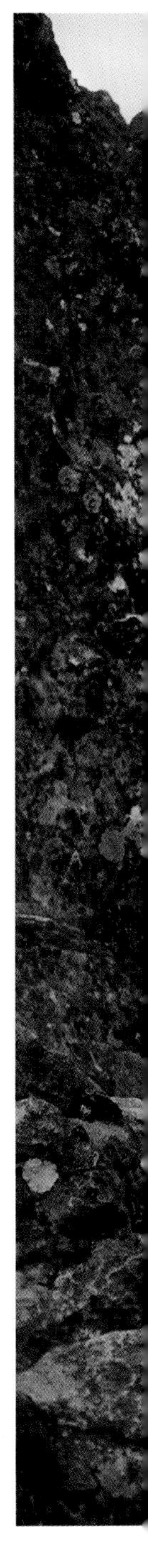

Hanging Rock 1900 #3
2006

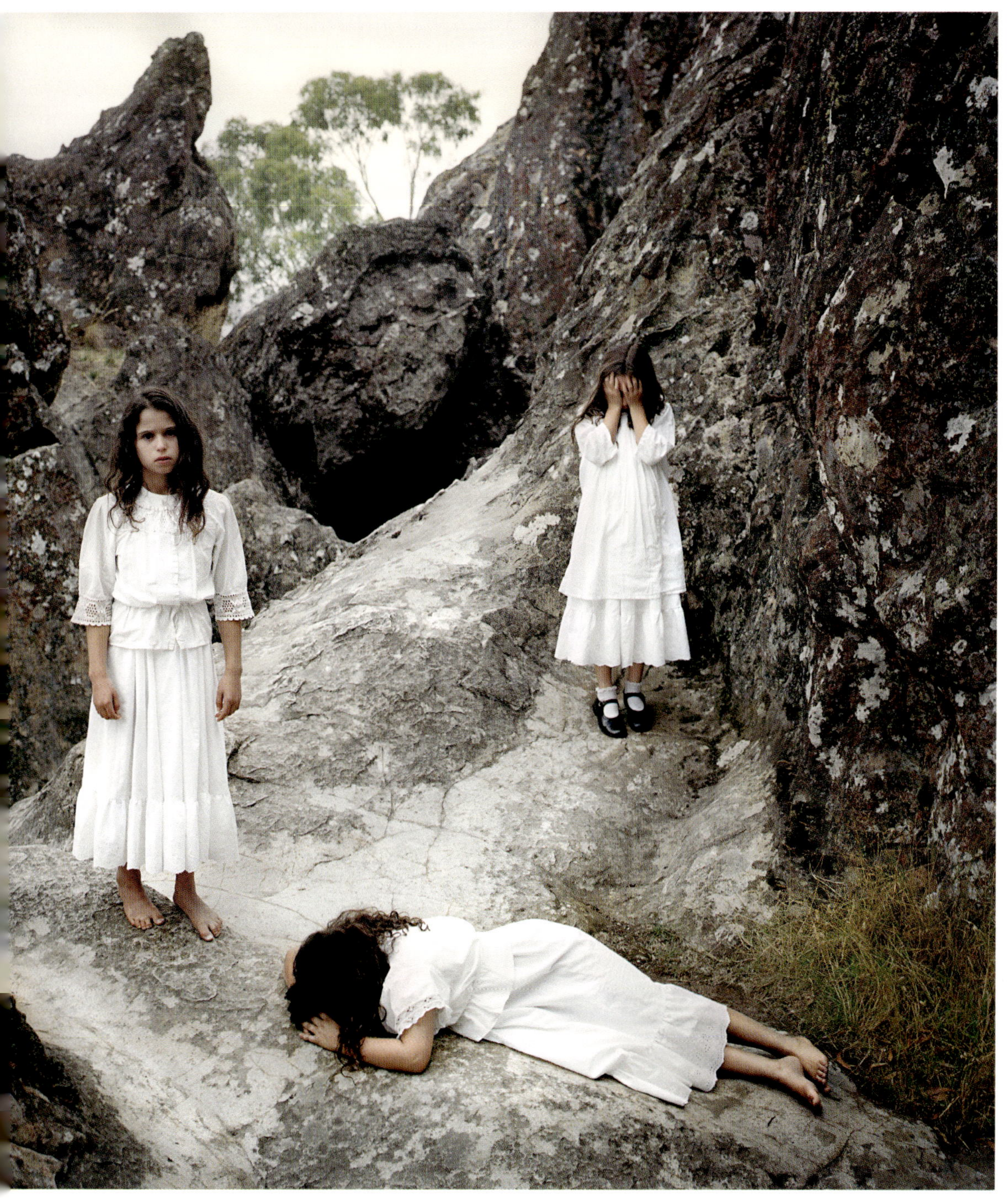

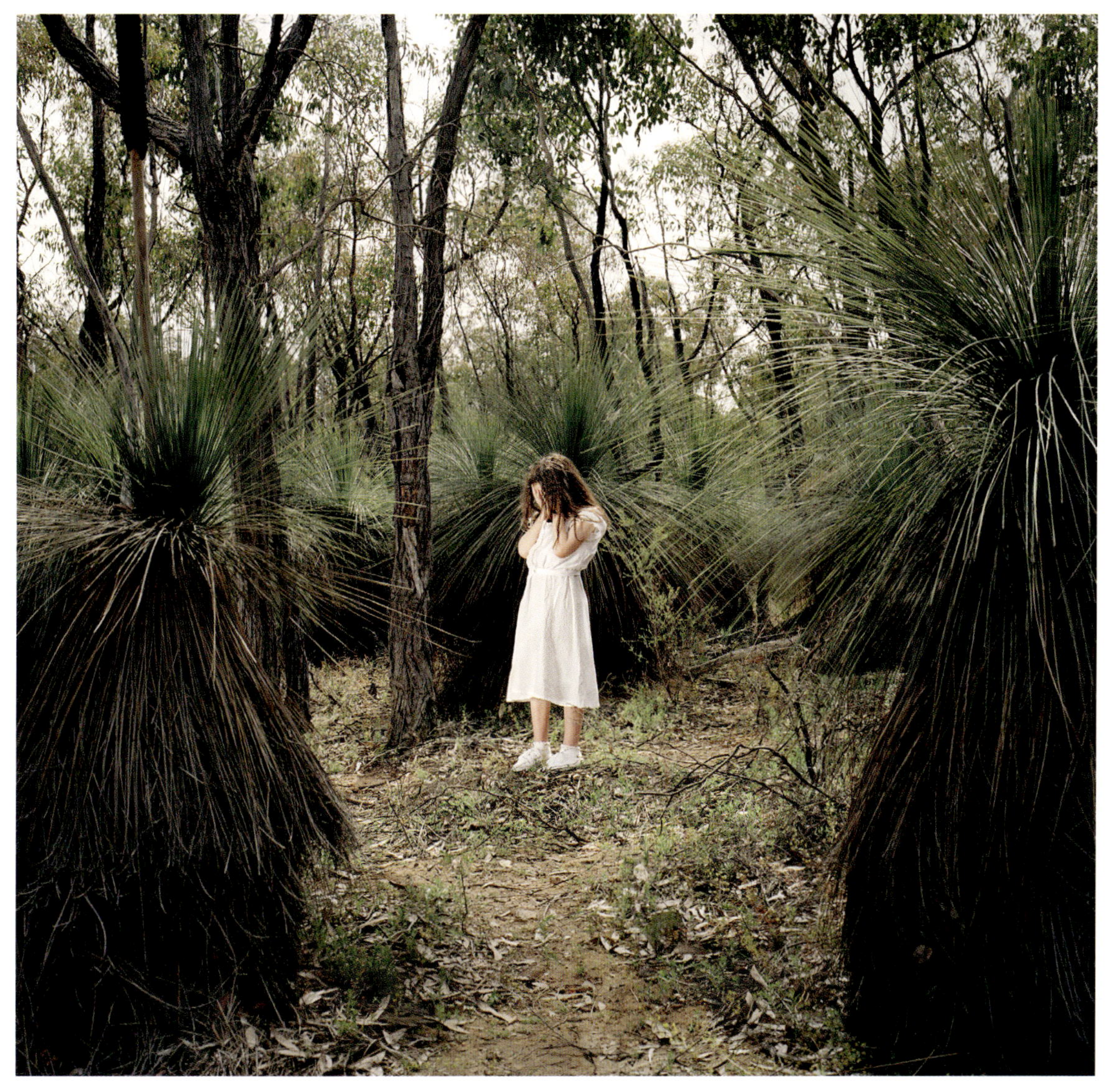

Witness 1933
2006

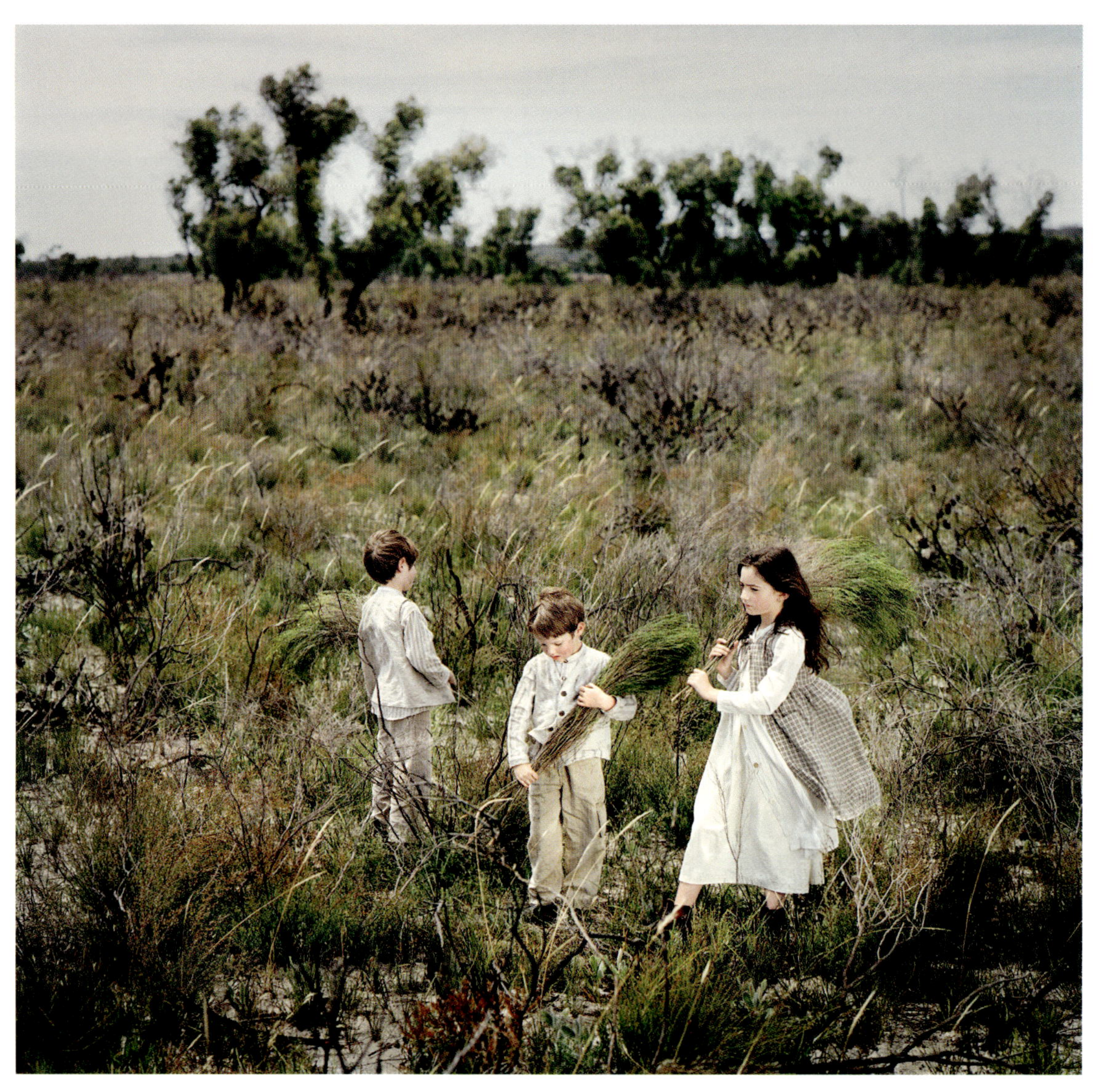

The Wimmera 1864 #1
2006

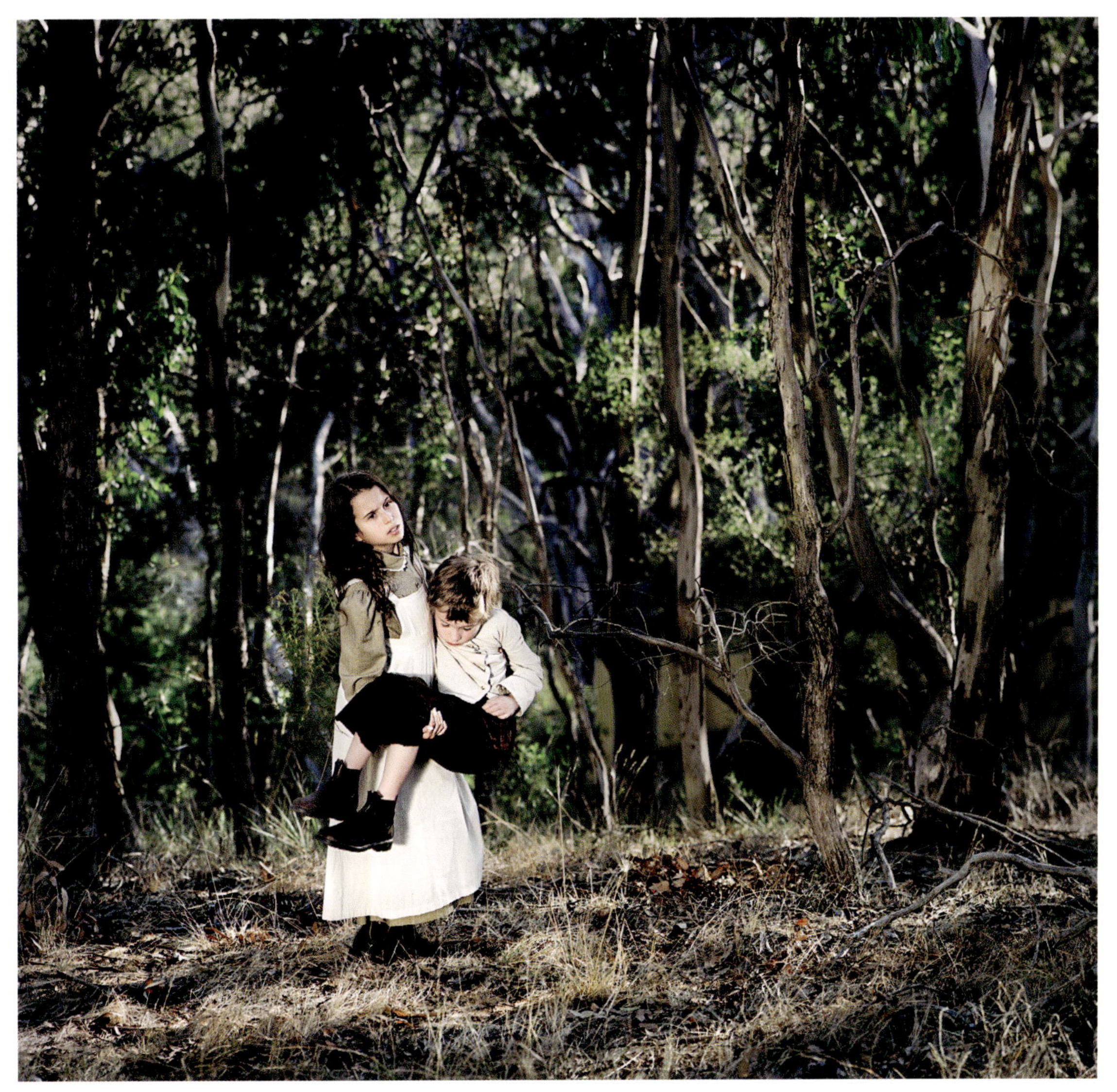

By the Yarra 1857 #2
2006

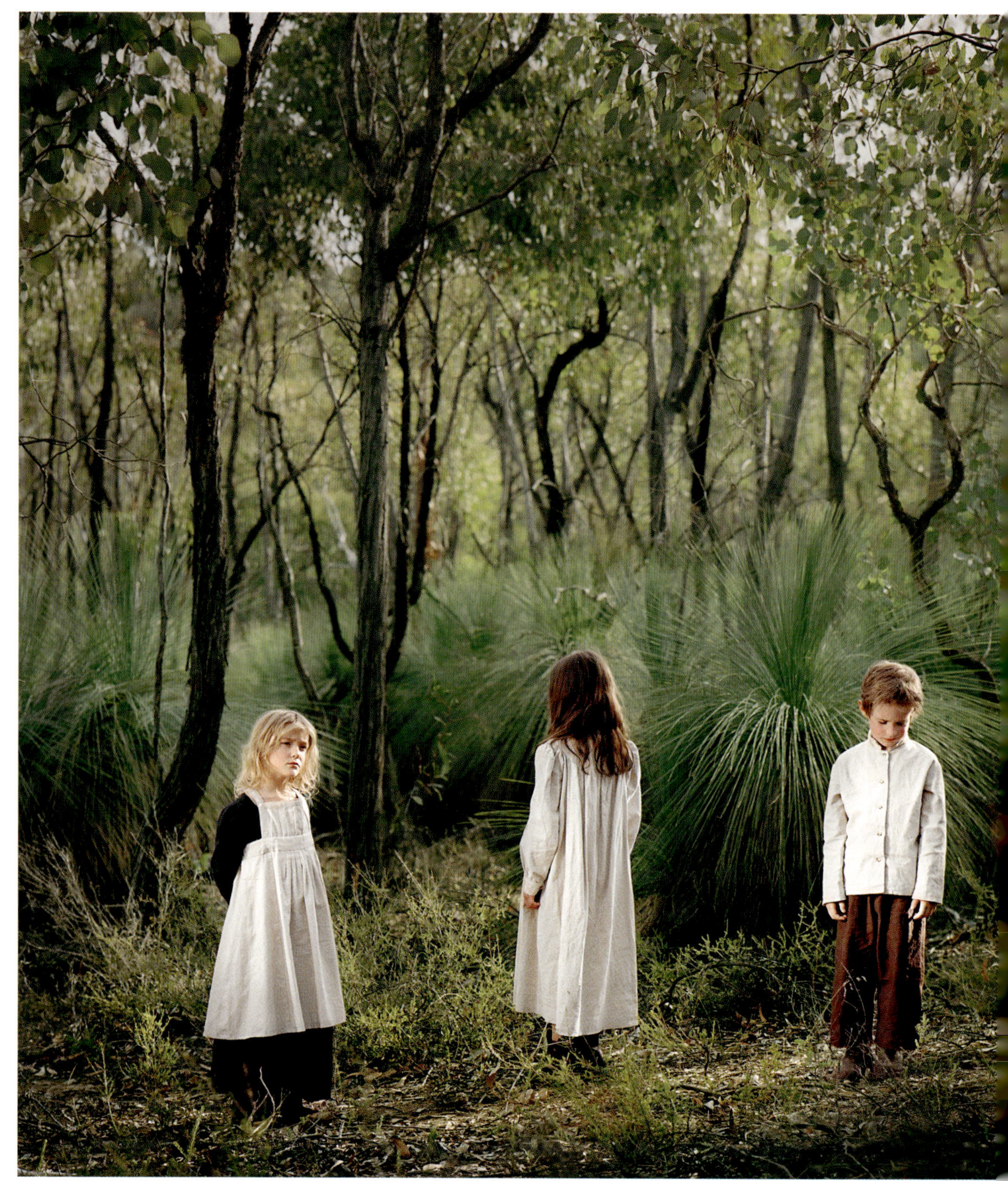

Whroo 1855
2006

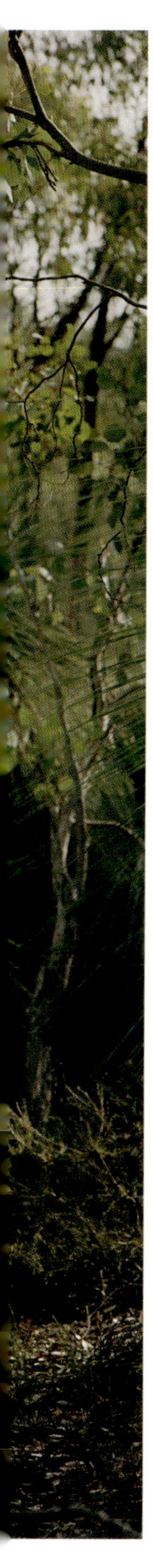

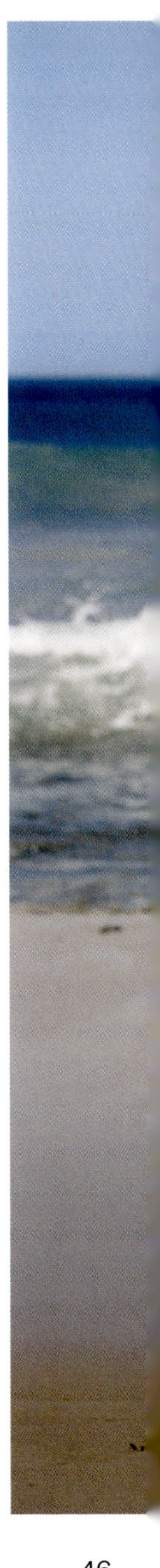

She saw two girls and a boy 1966 #1
2006

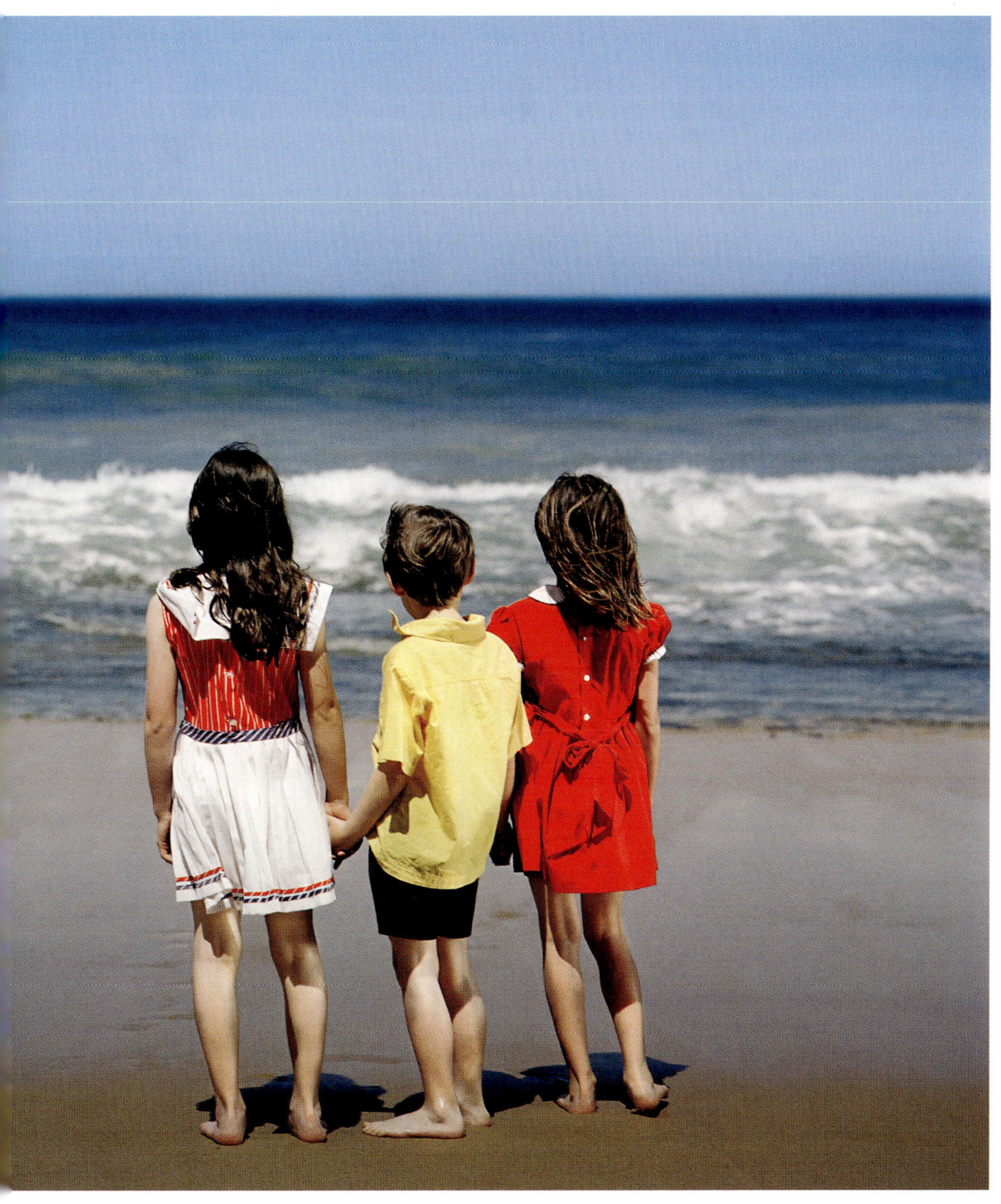

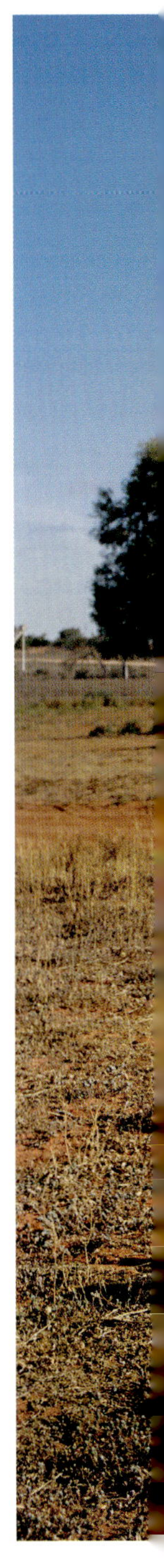

Miles from nowhere
2008

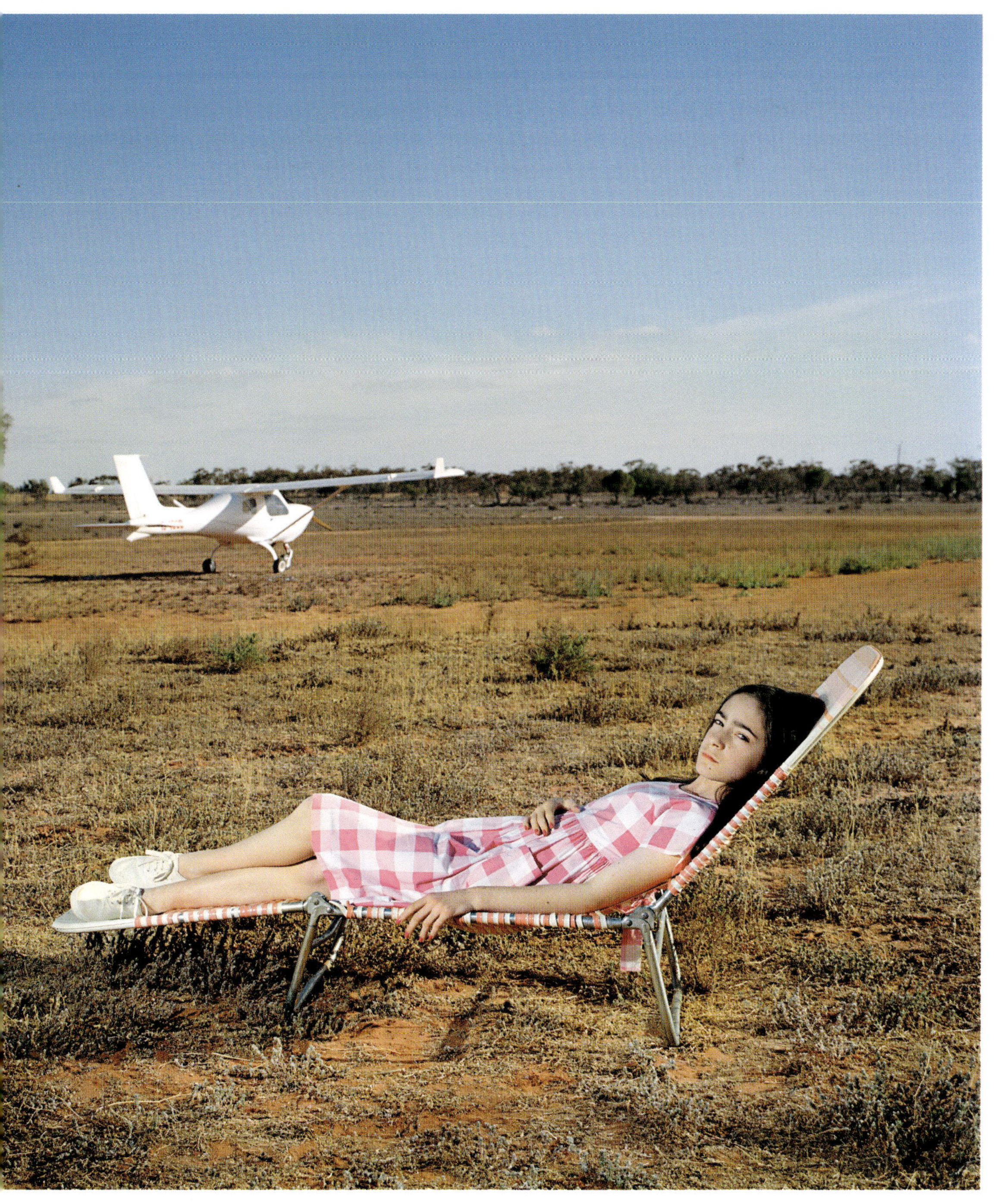

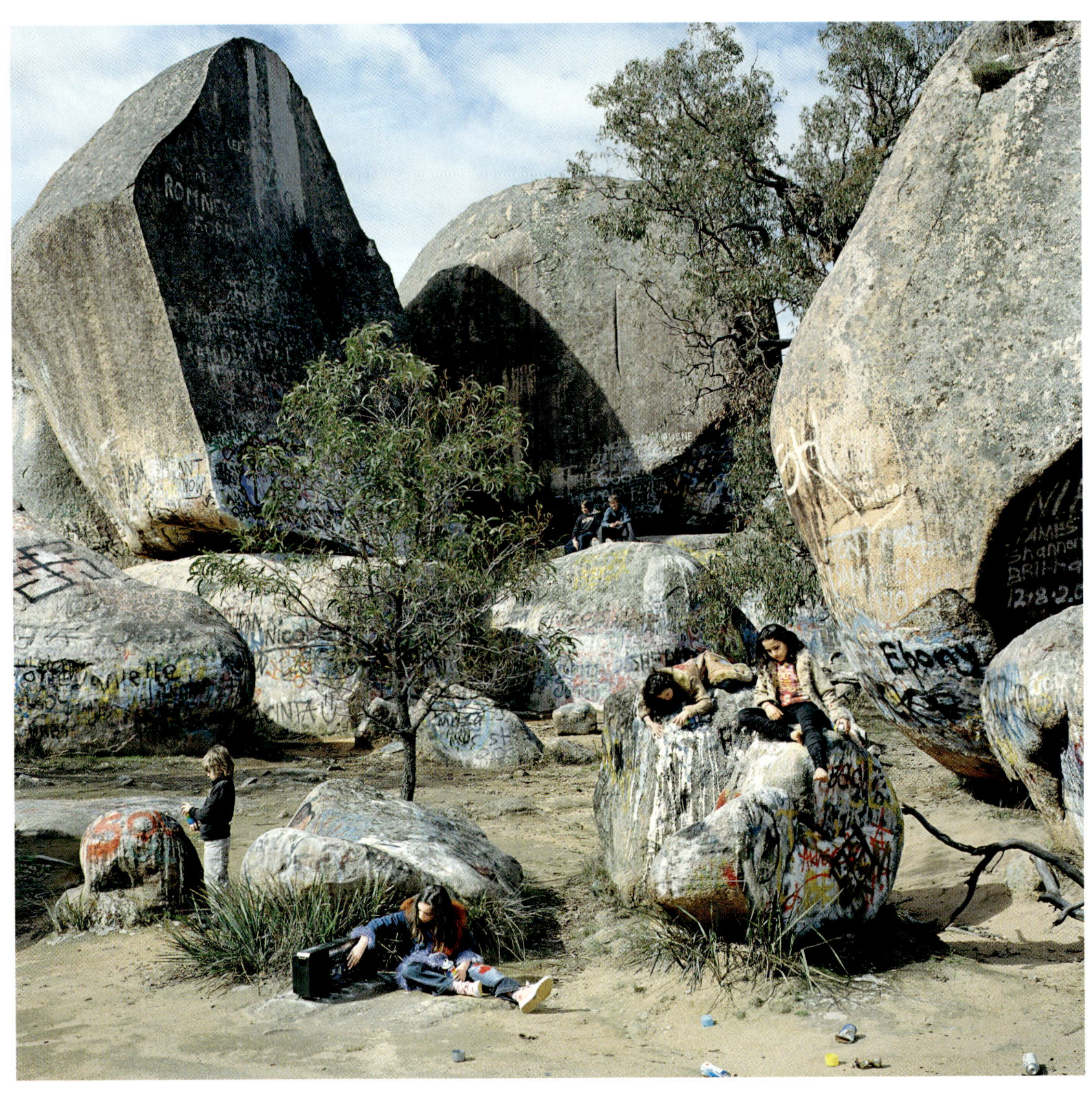

Sisters Rocks
2008

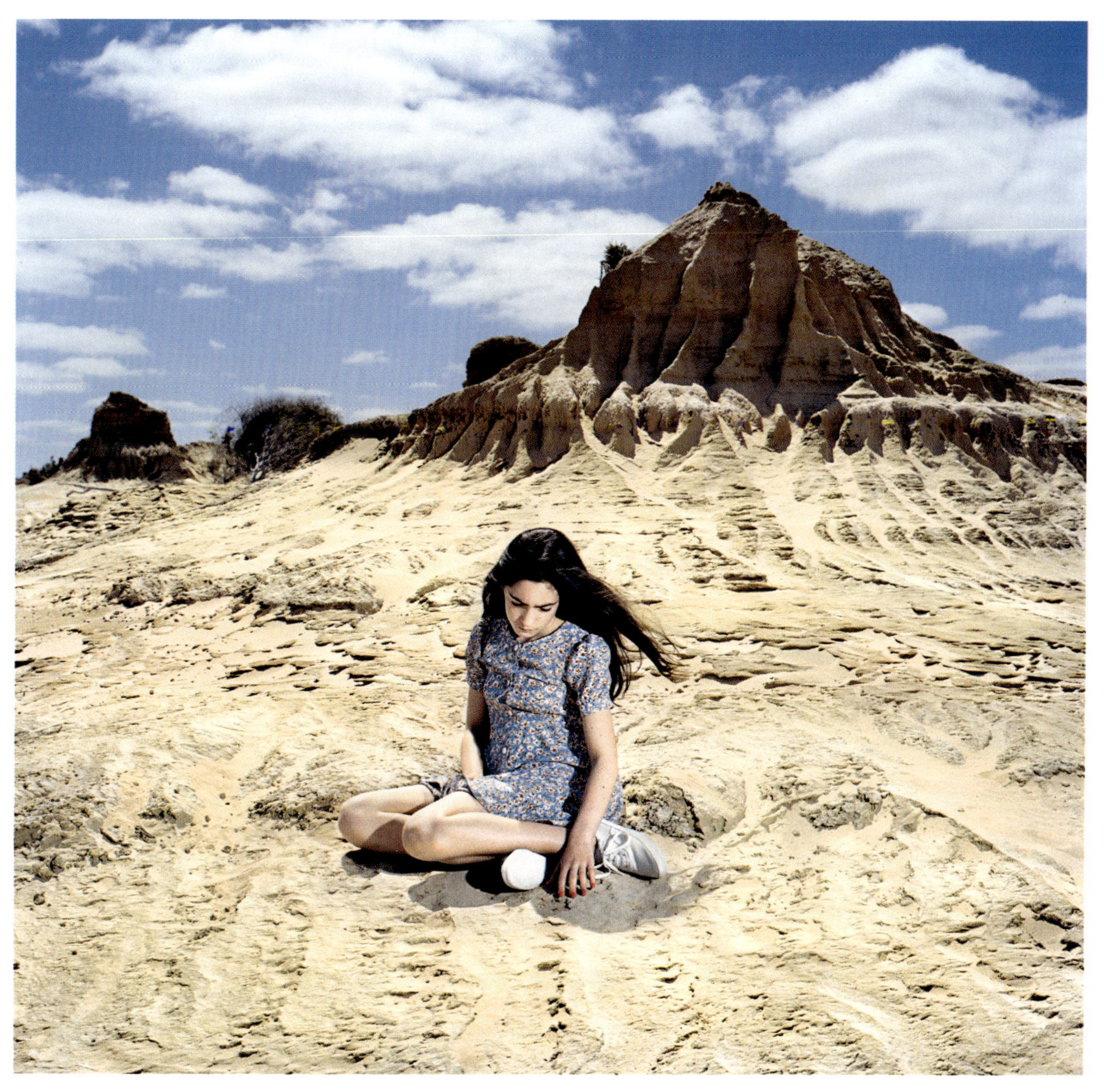

Wild World
2008

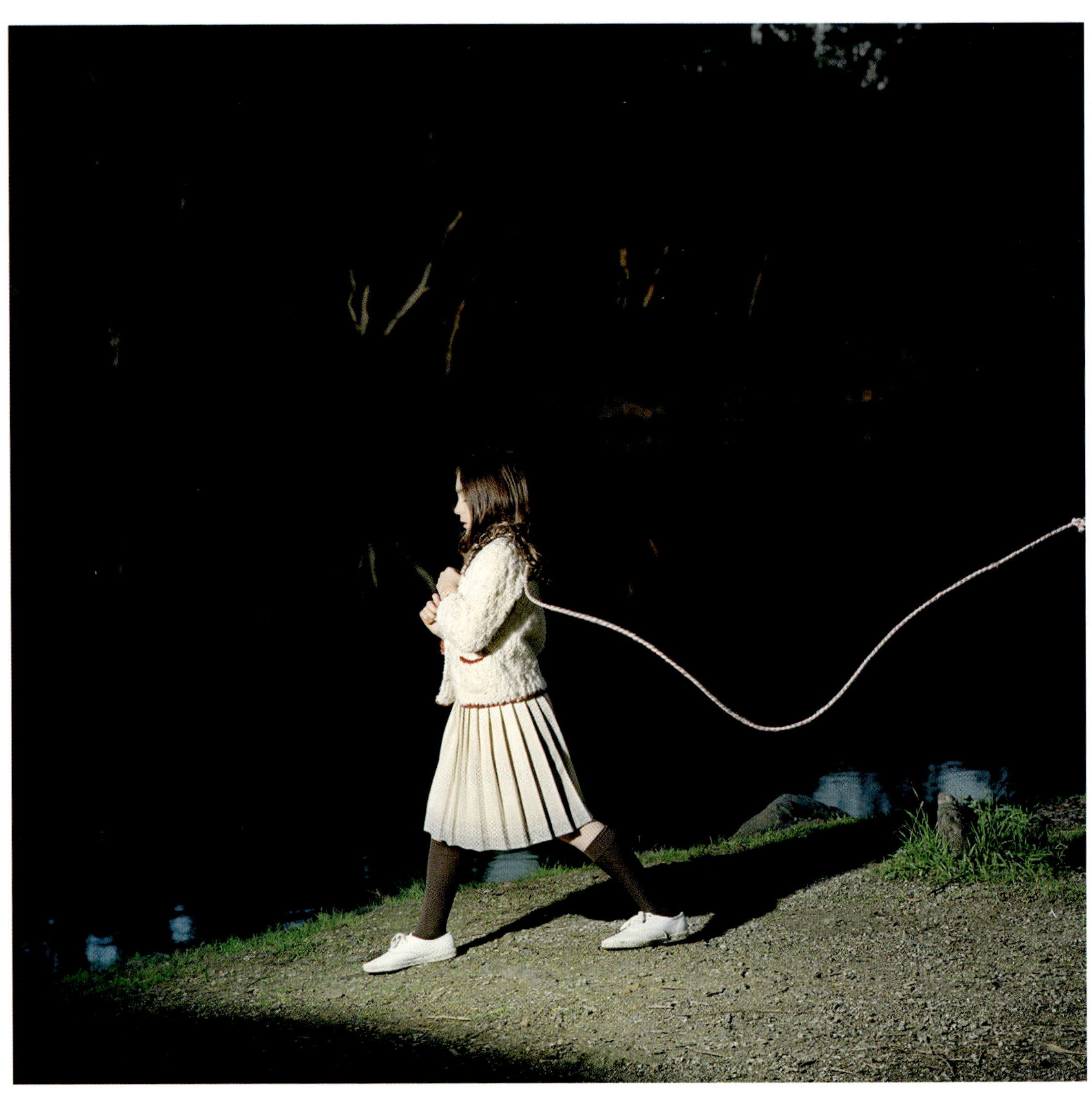

Dreams are like water
2008

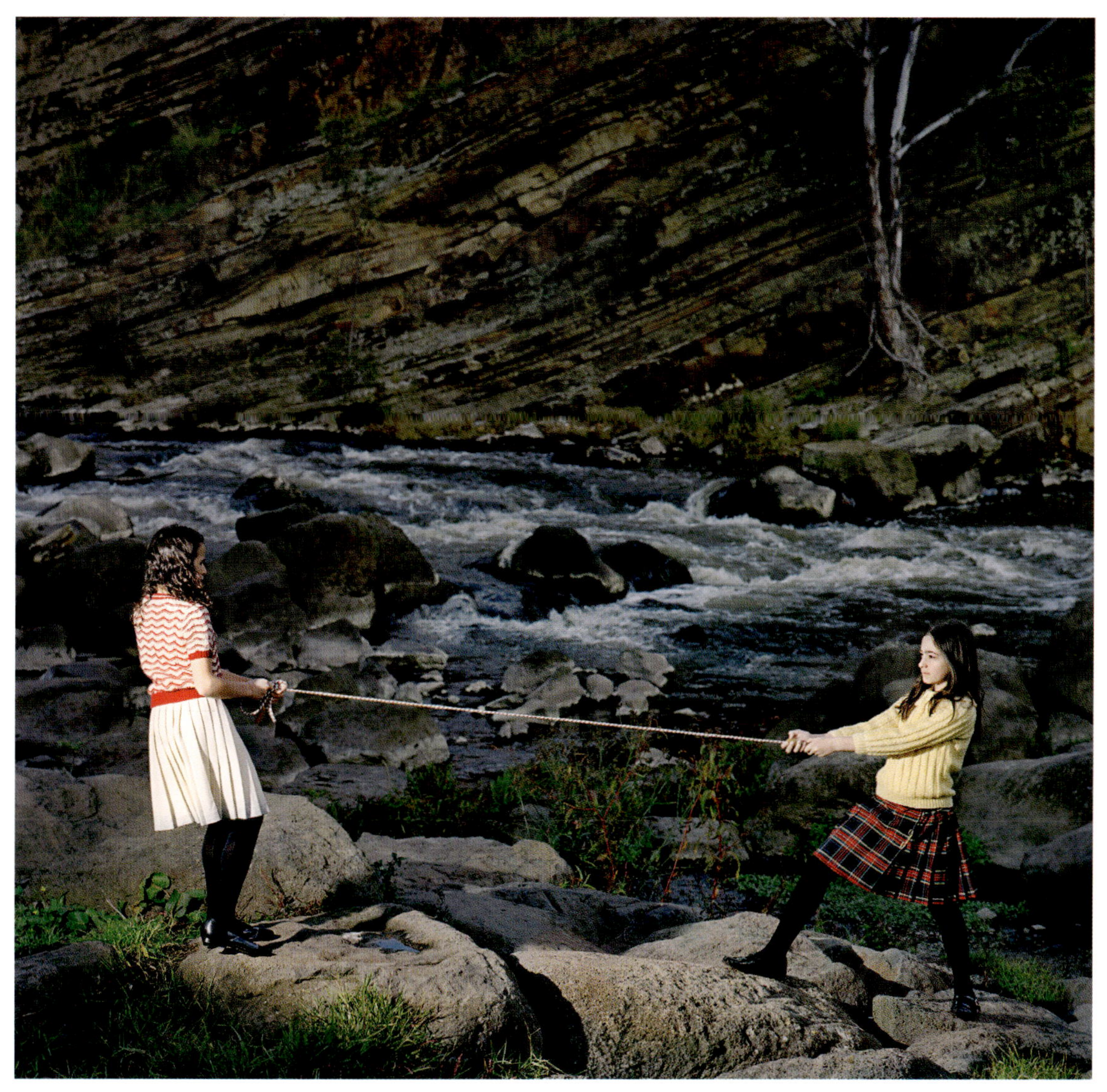

Dights Falls
2008

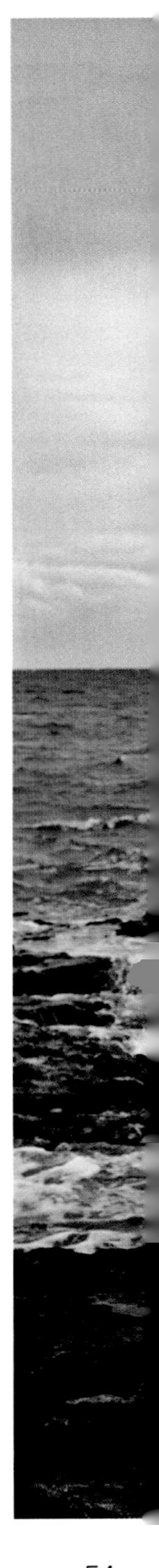

The Wave Counter
2011

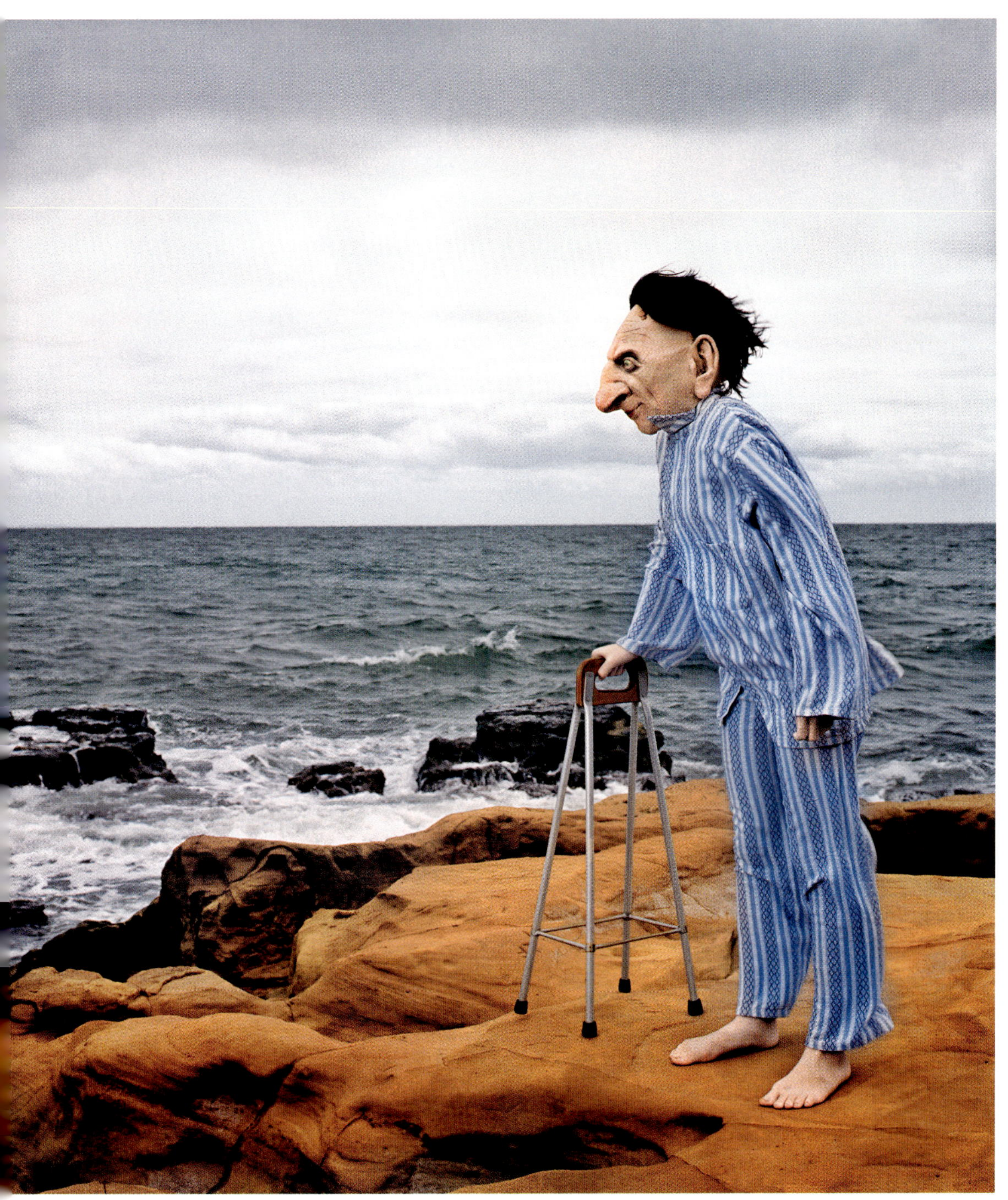

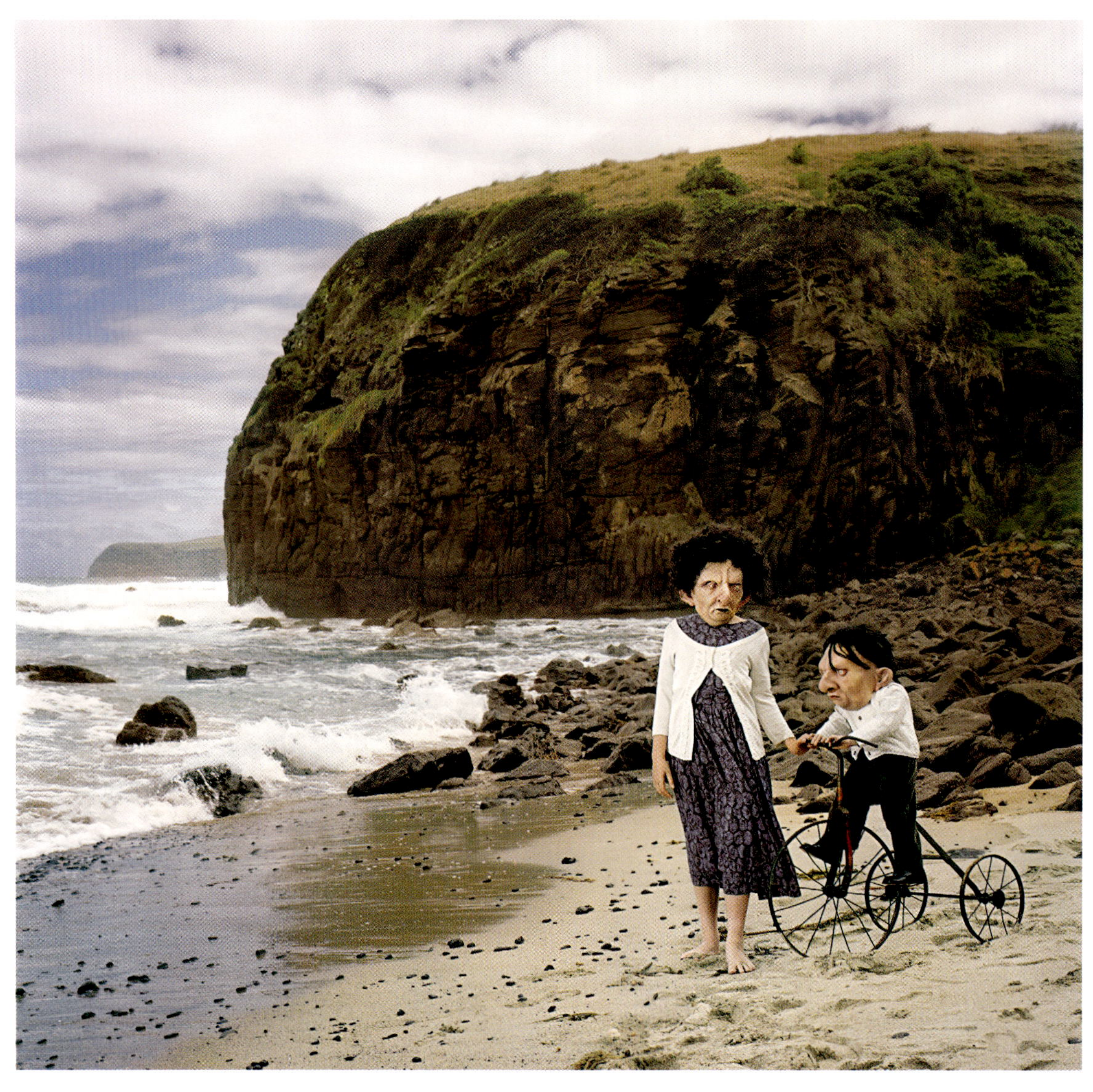

The Shell Collectors
2012

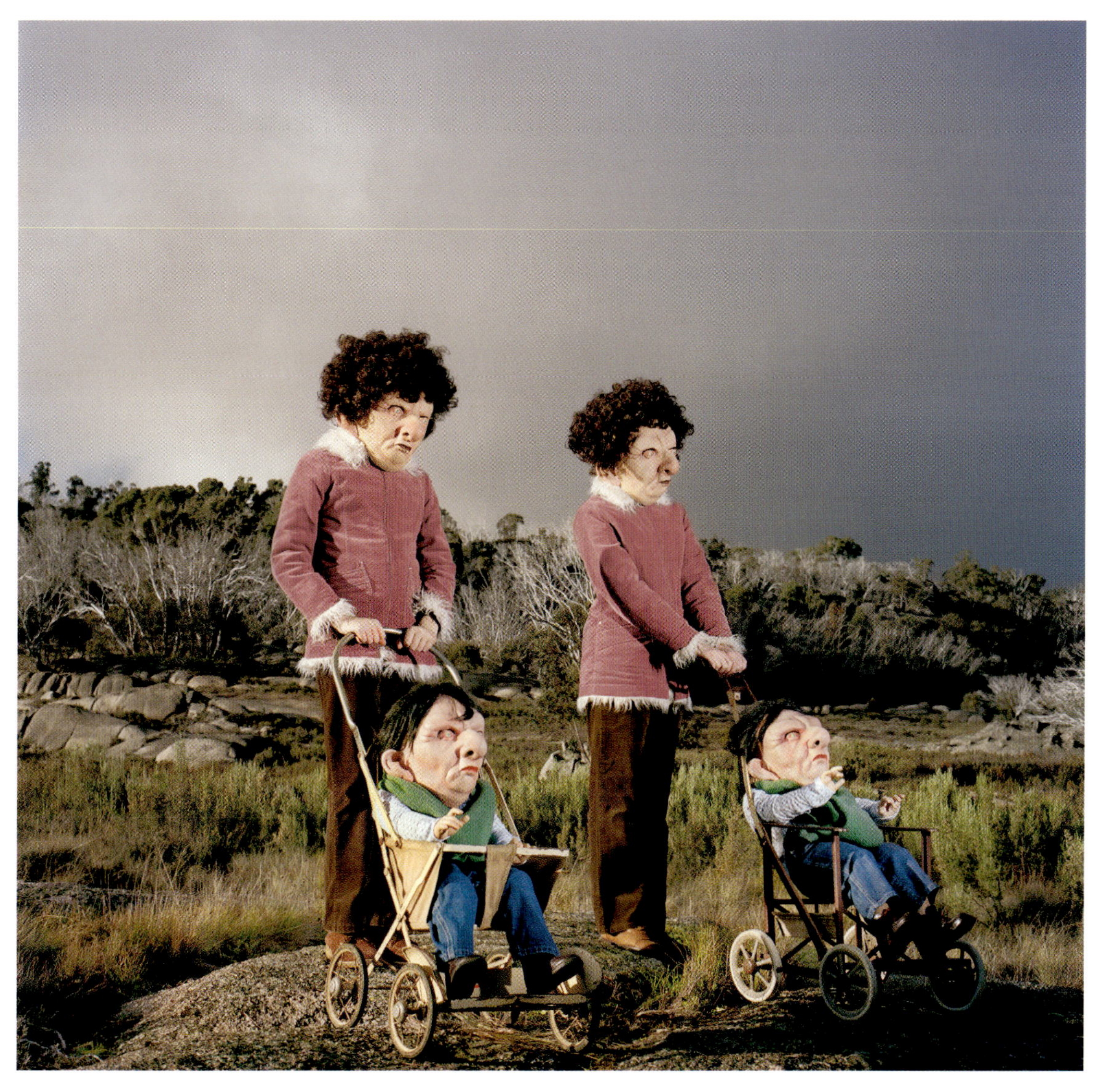

The Mystical Mothers
2011

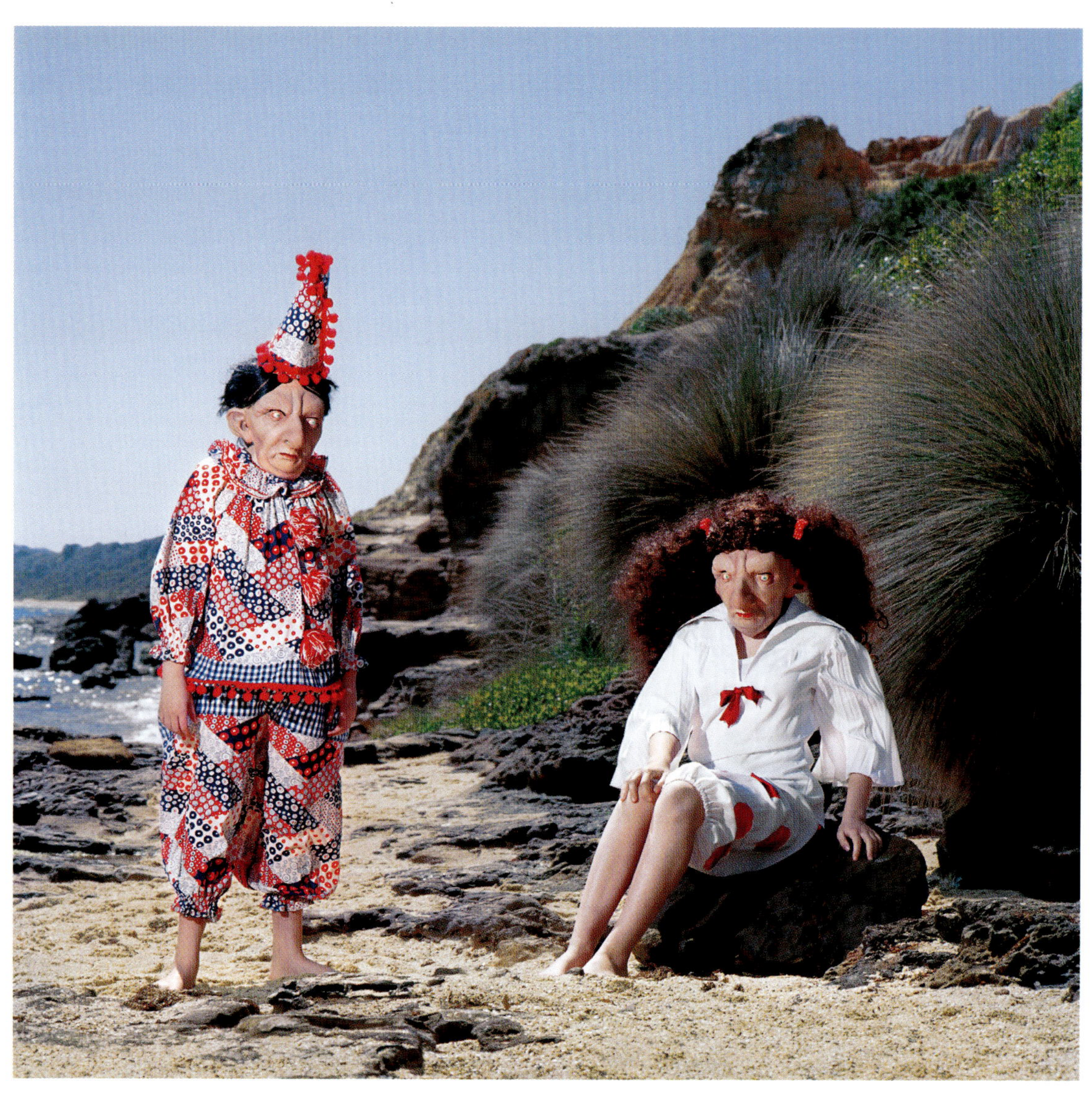

The Joy Pedlars
2011

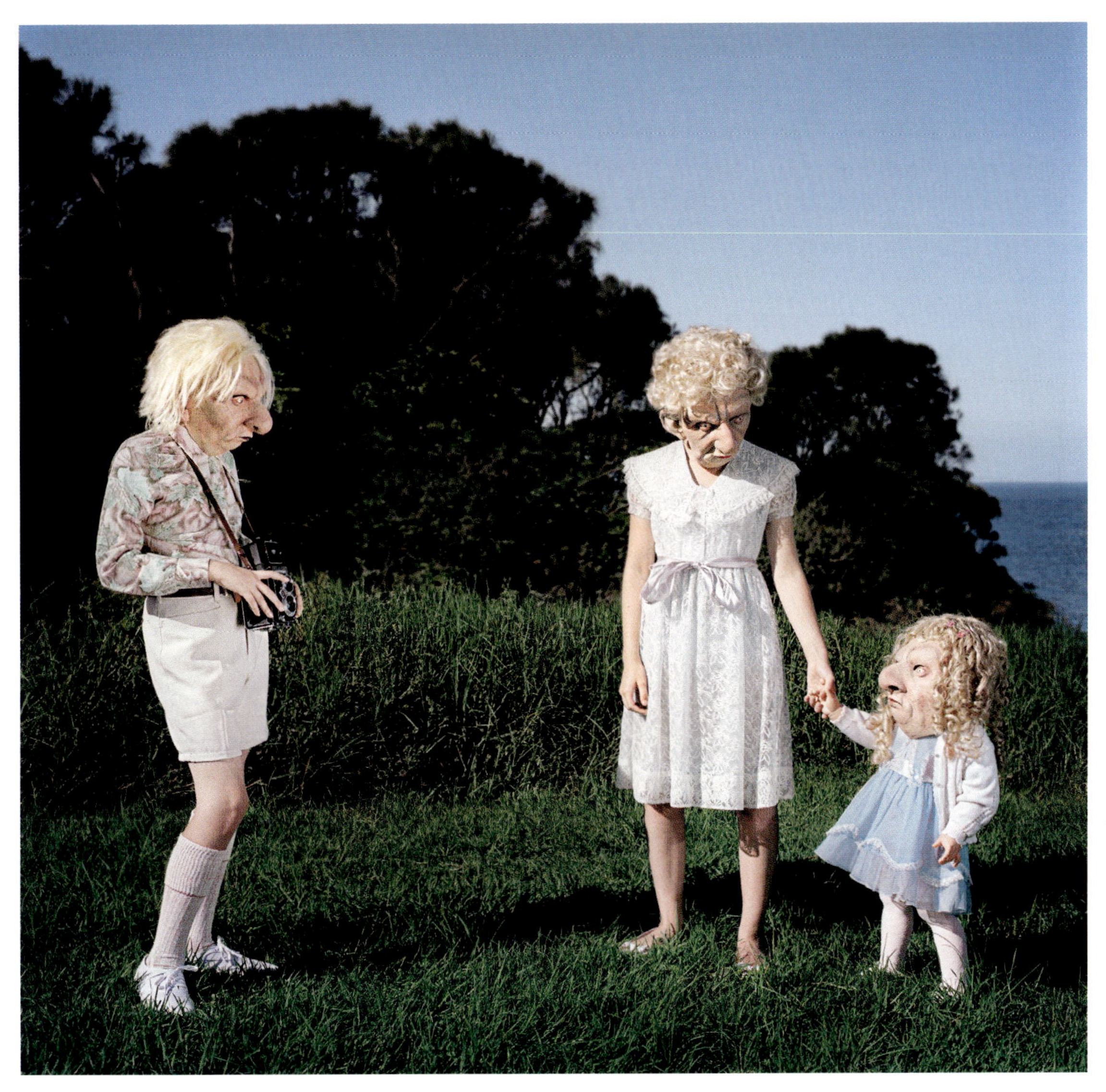

The Holiday Makers
2011

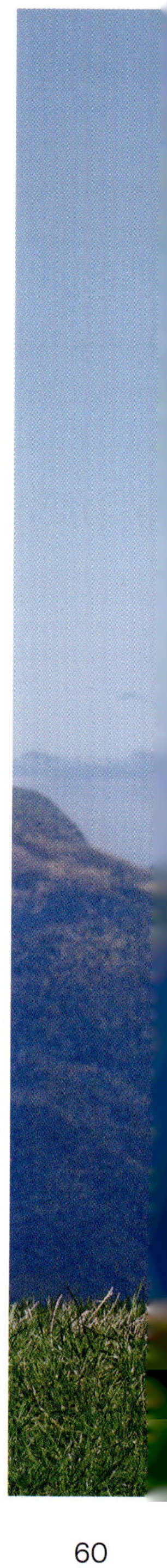

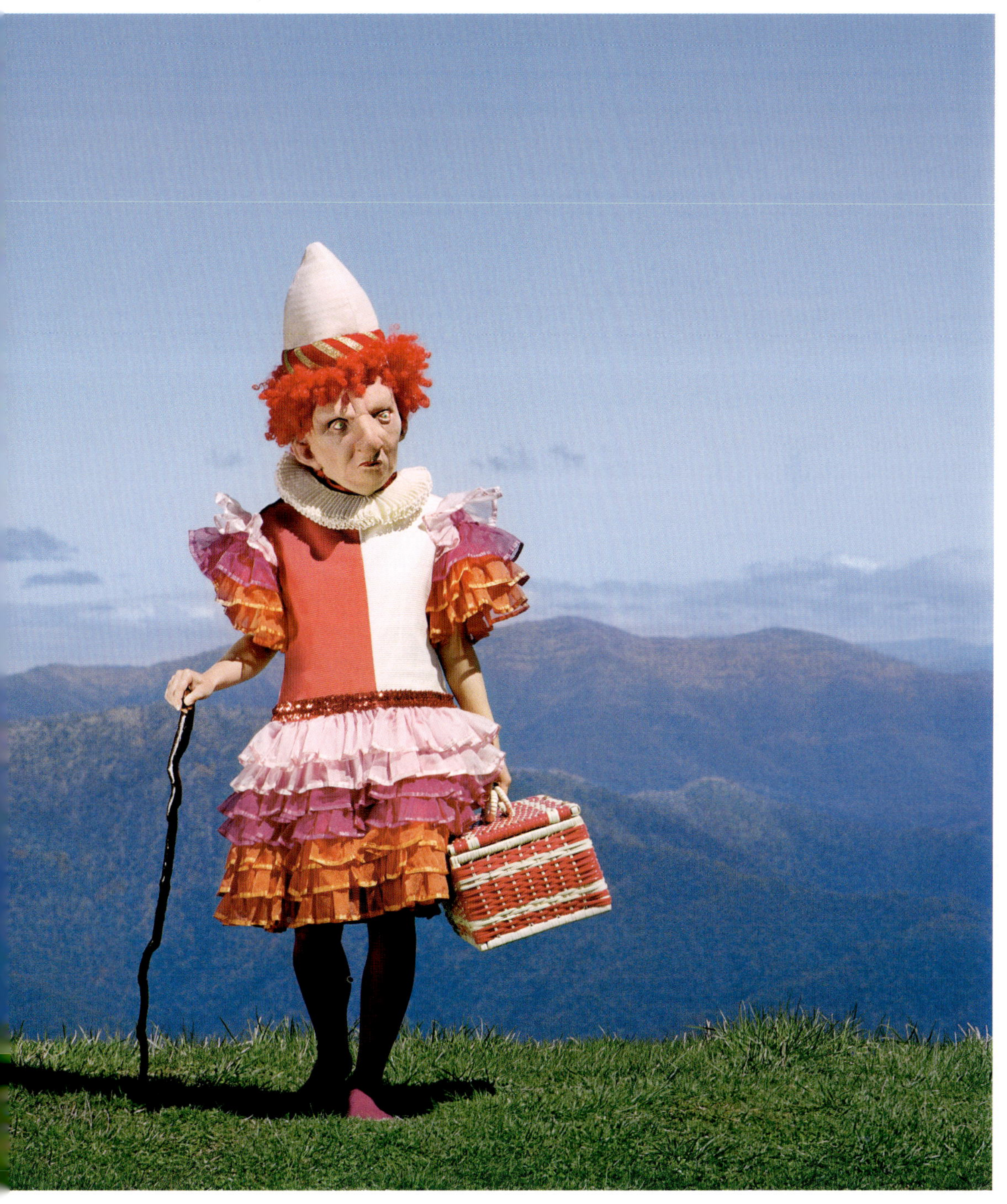

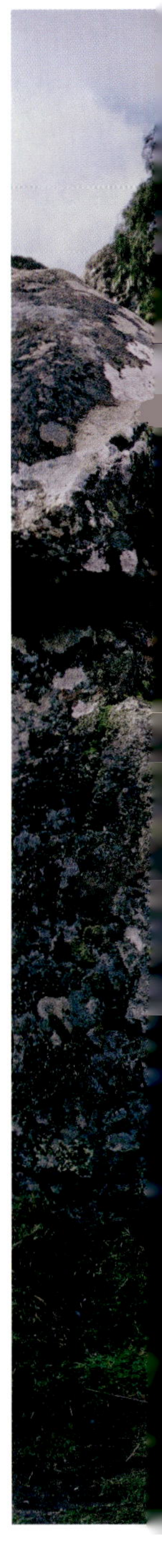

The Lantern Keeper
2012

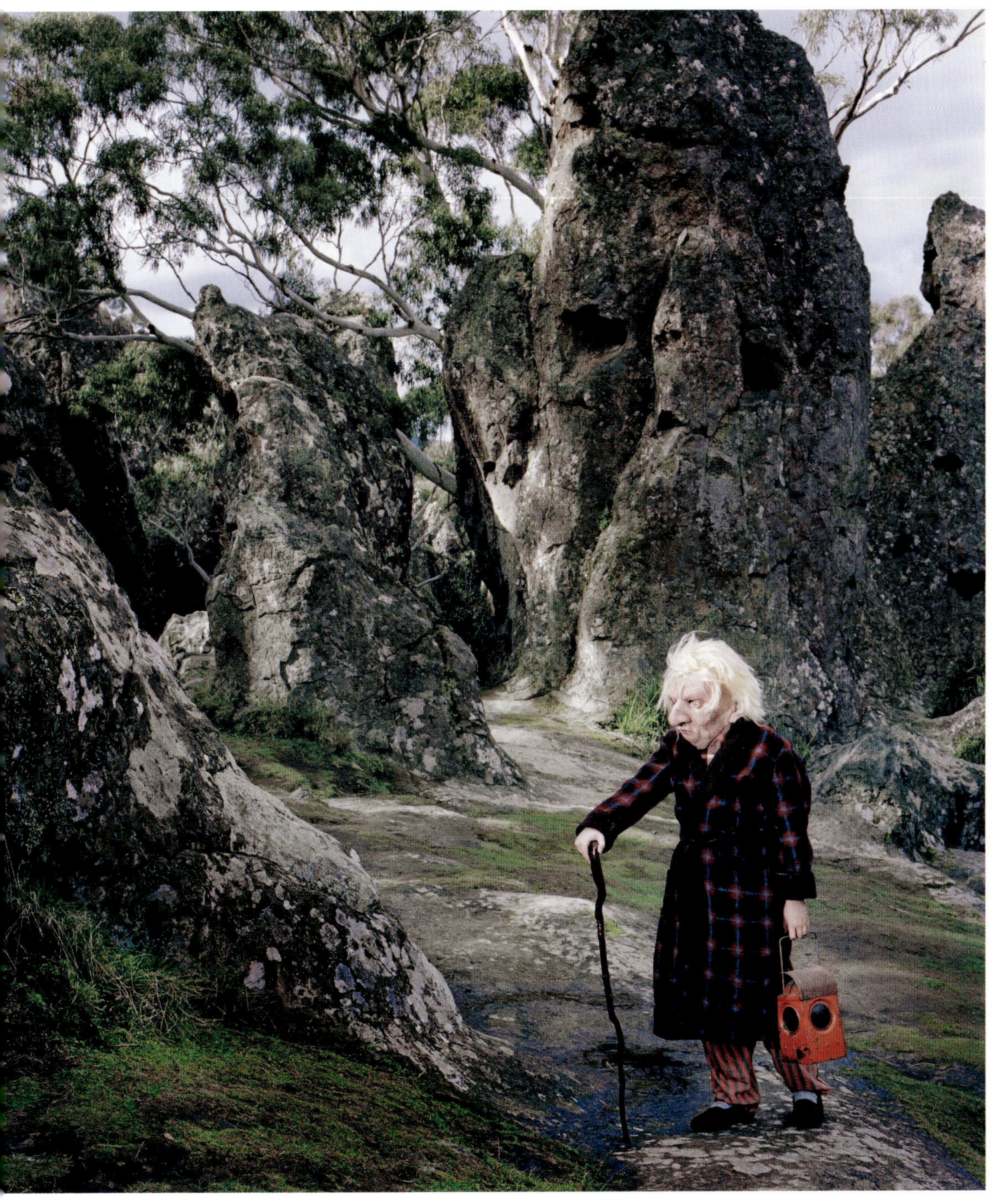

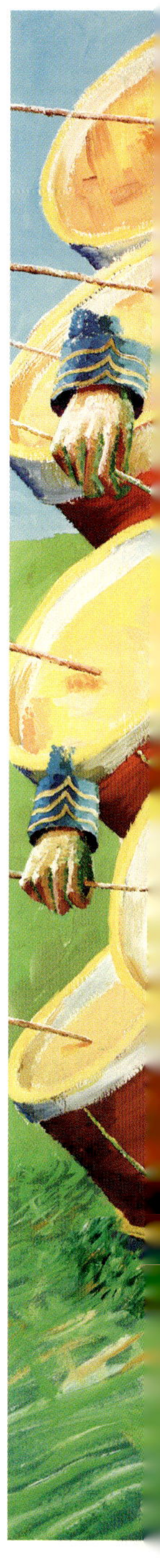

The Beating Drums
2003

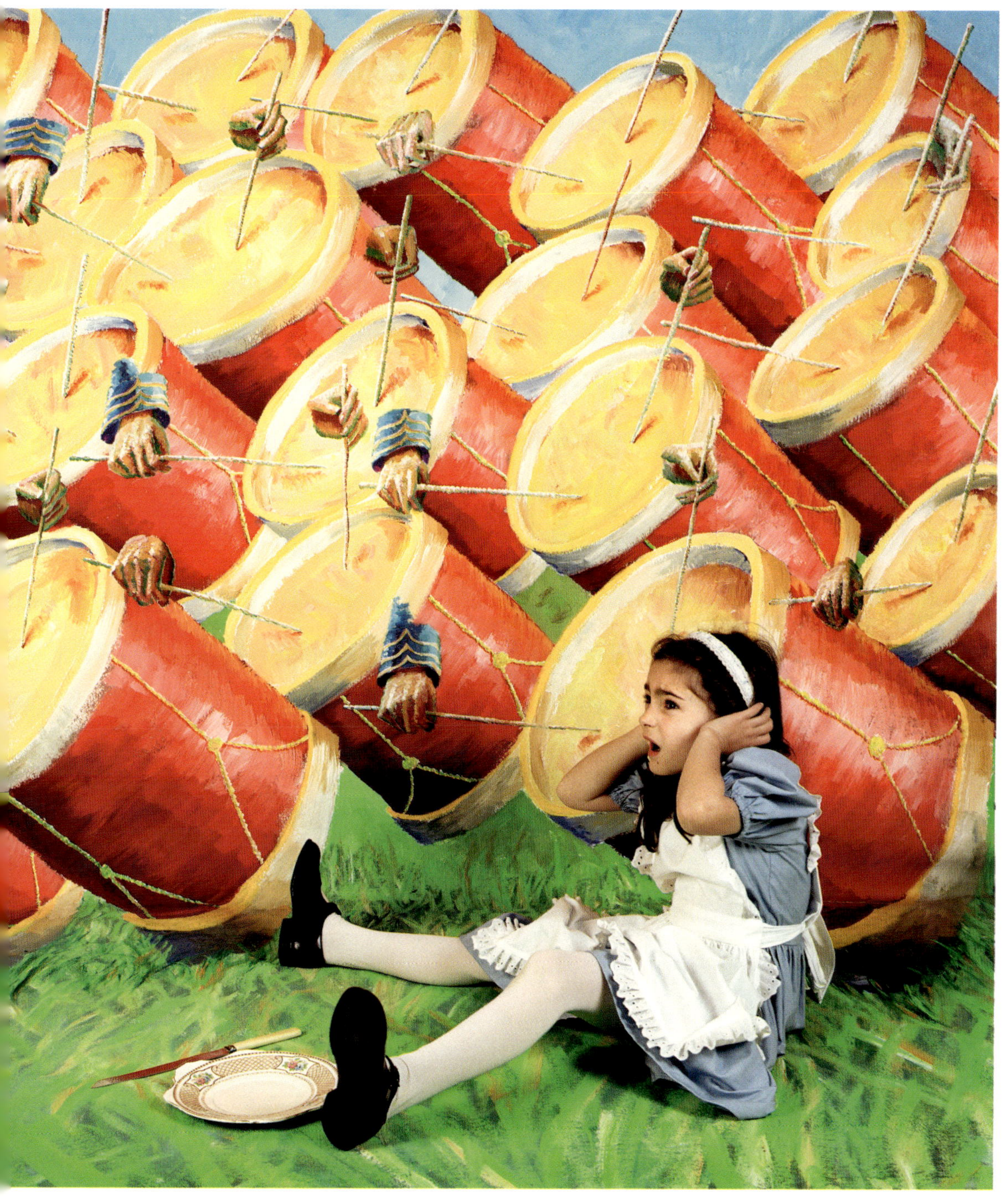

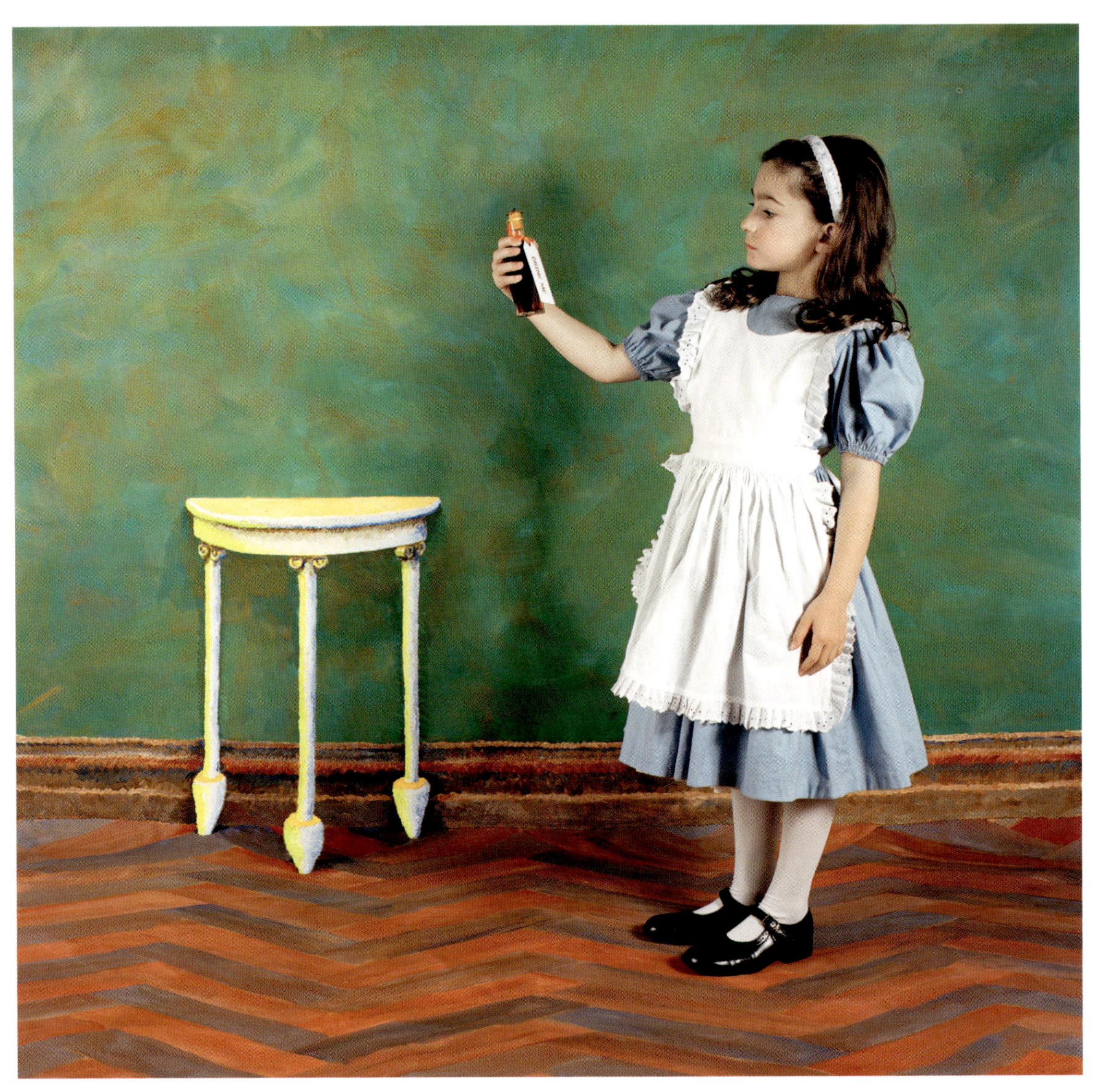

Drink Me
2004

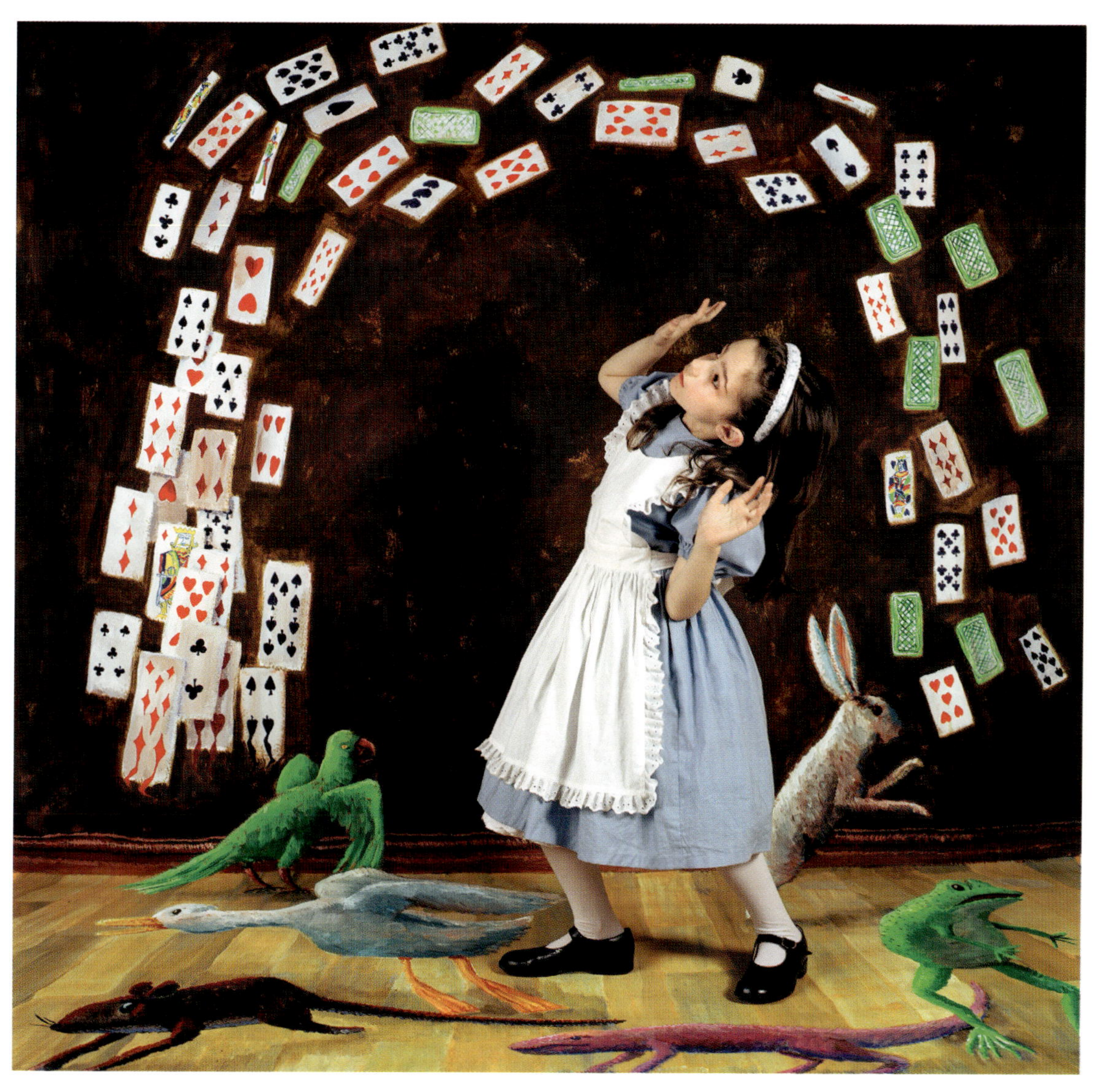

Flying Cards #2
2004

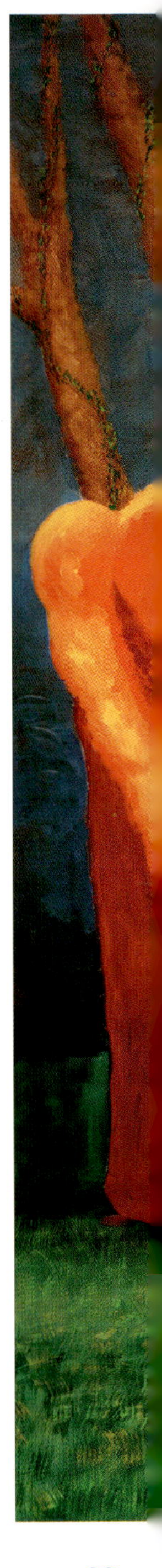

Riddles that have no answers
2004

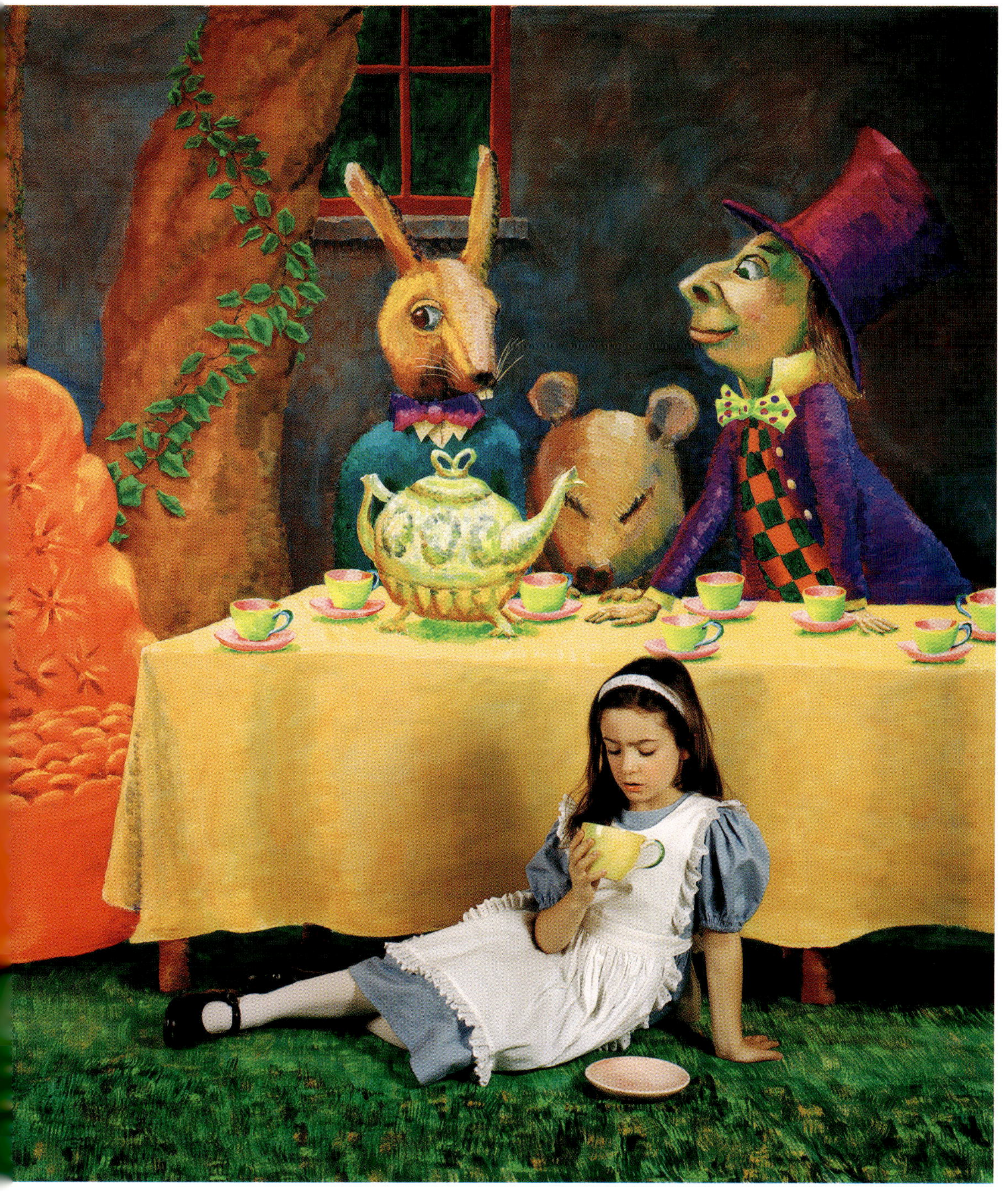

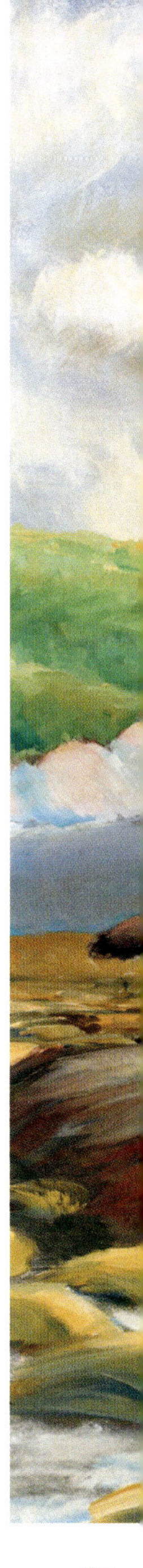

Olympia as Lewis Carroll's Beatrice Hatch before White Cliffs
2003

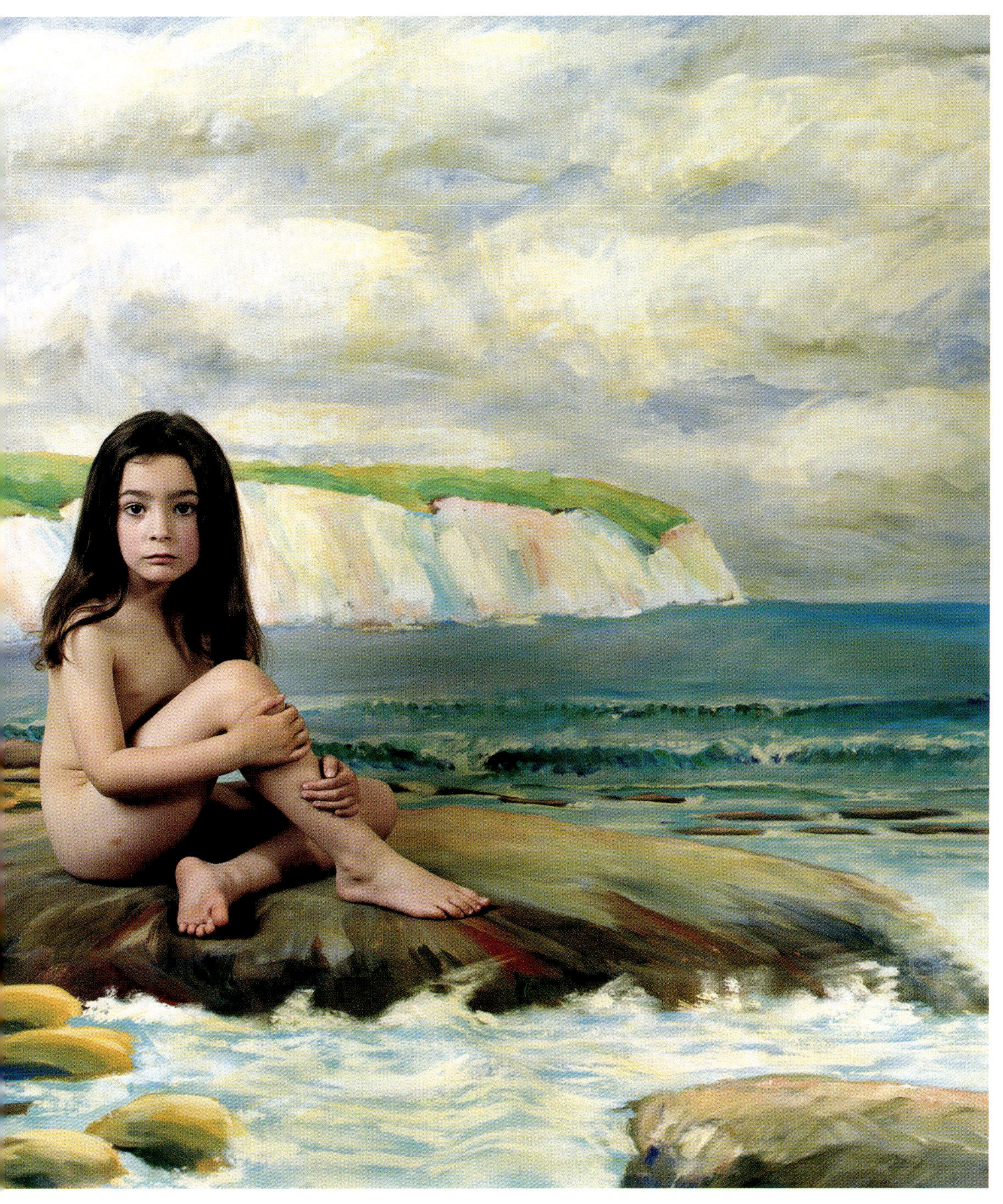

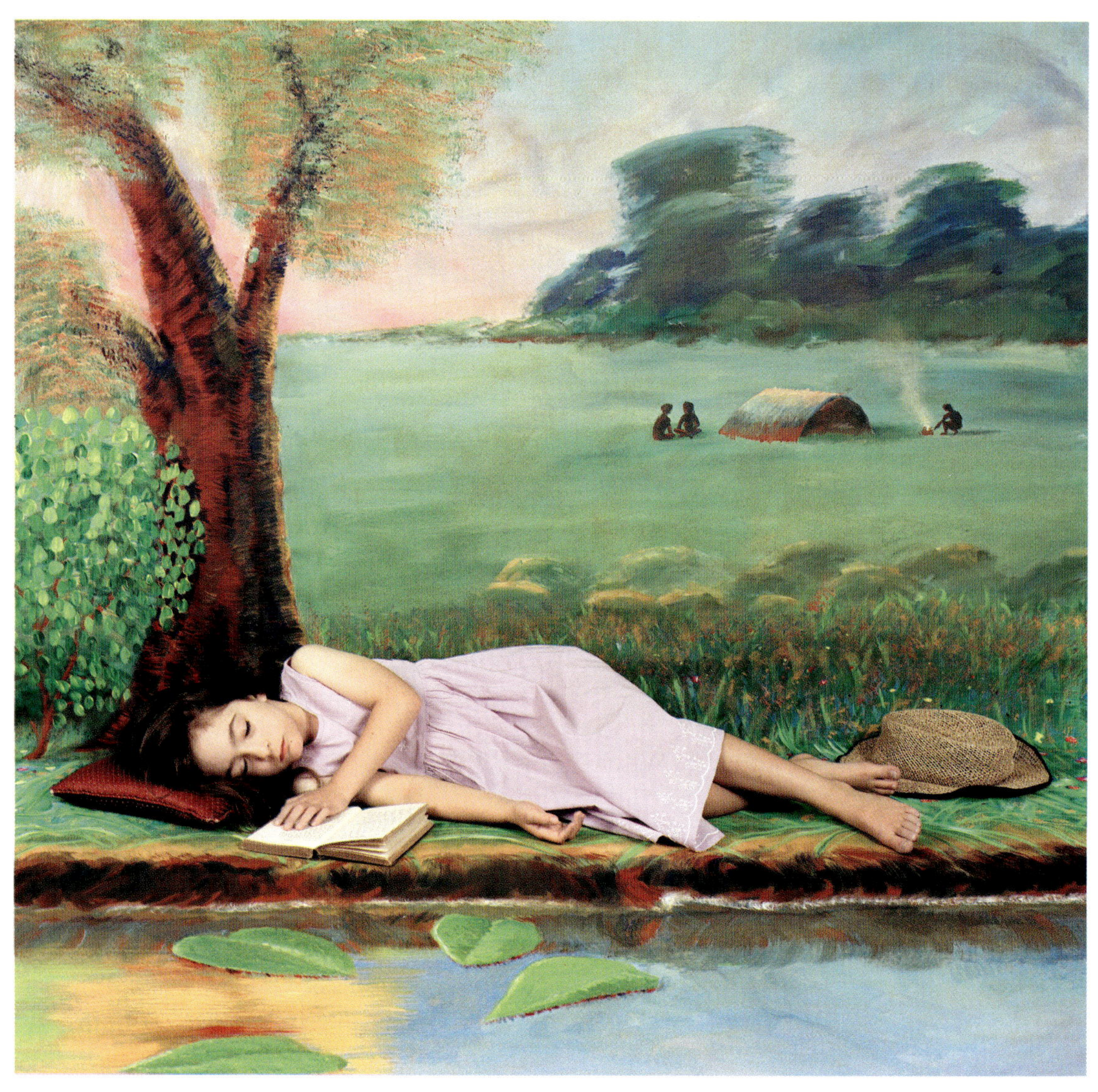

Olympia as Alice dreaming by the Riverbank
2003

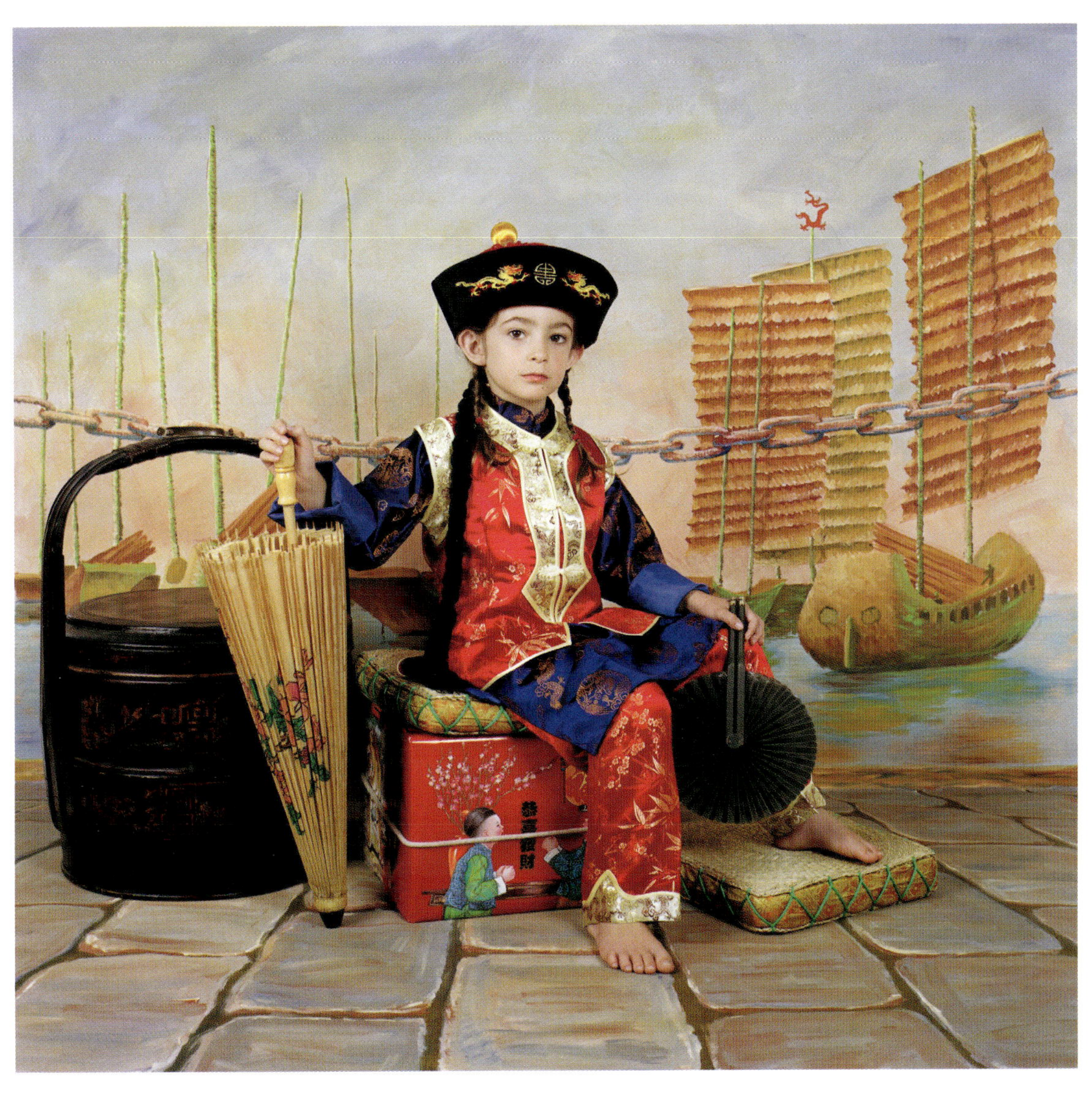

Olympia as Lewis Carroll's Xie Kitchin as a Chinaman (off duty)
2003

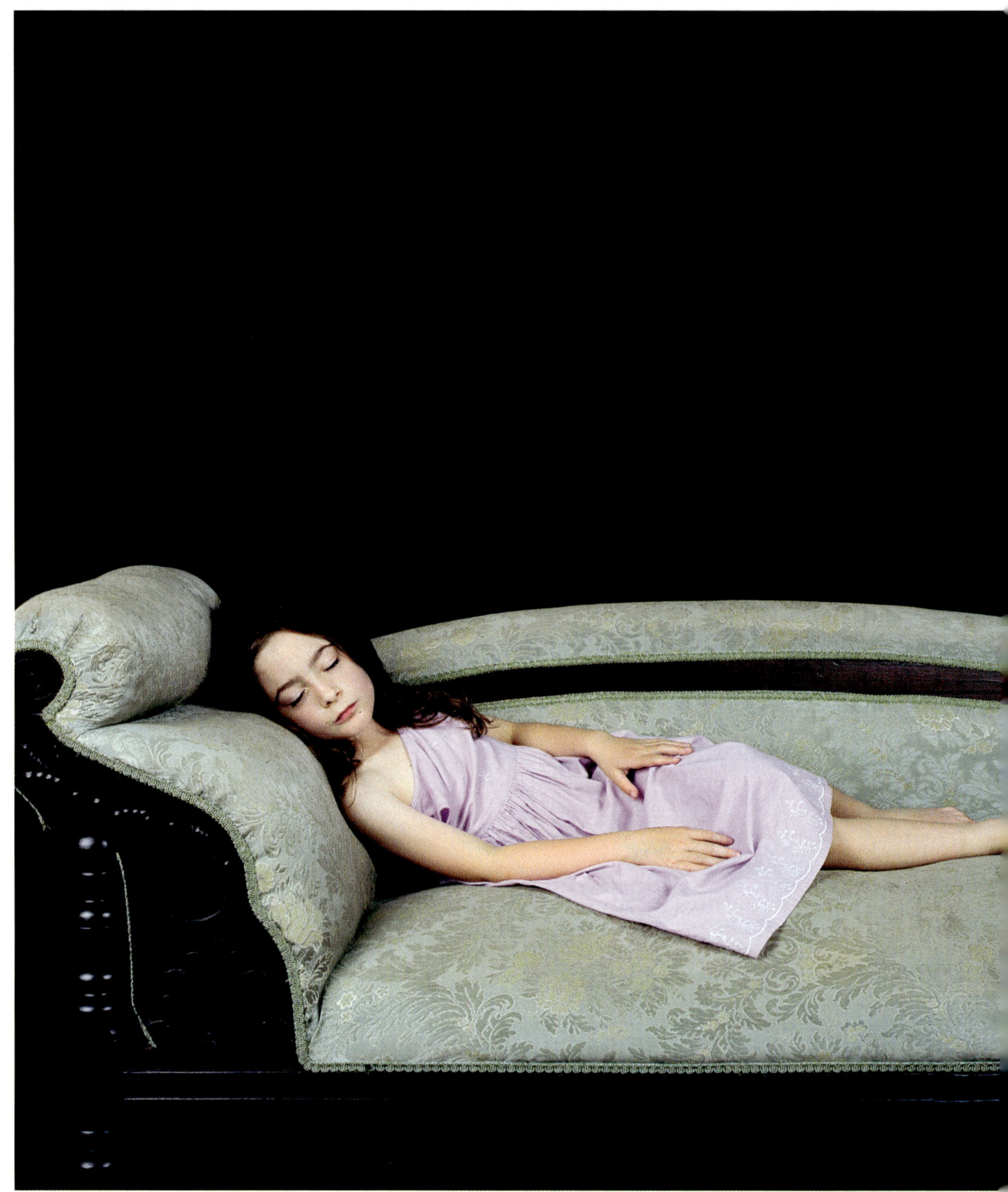

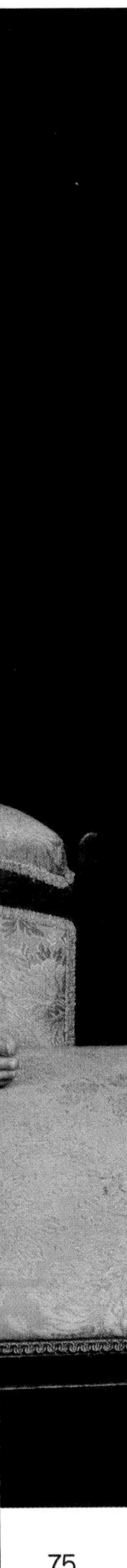

Olympia as Lewis Carroll's Xie Kitchin (sleeping on chaise)
2003

Melancholia
2014

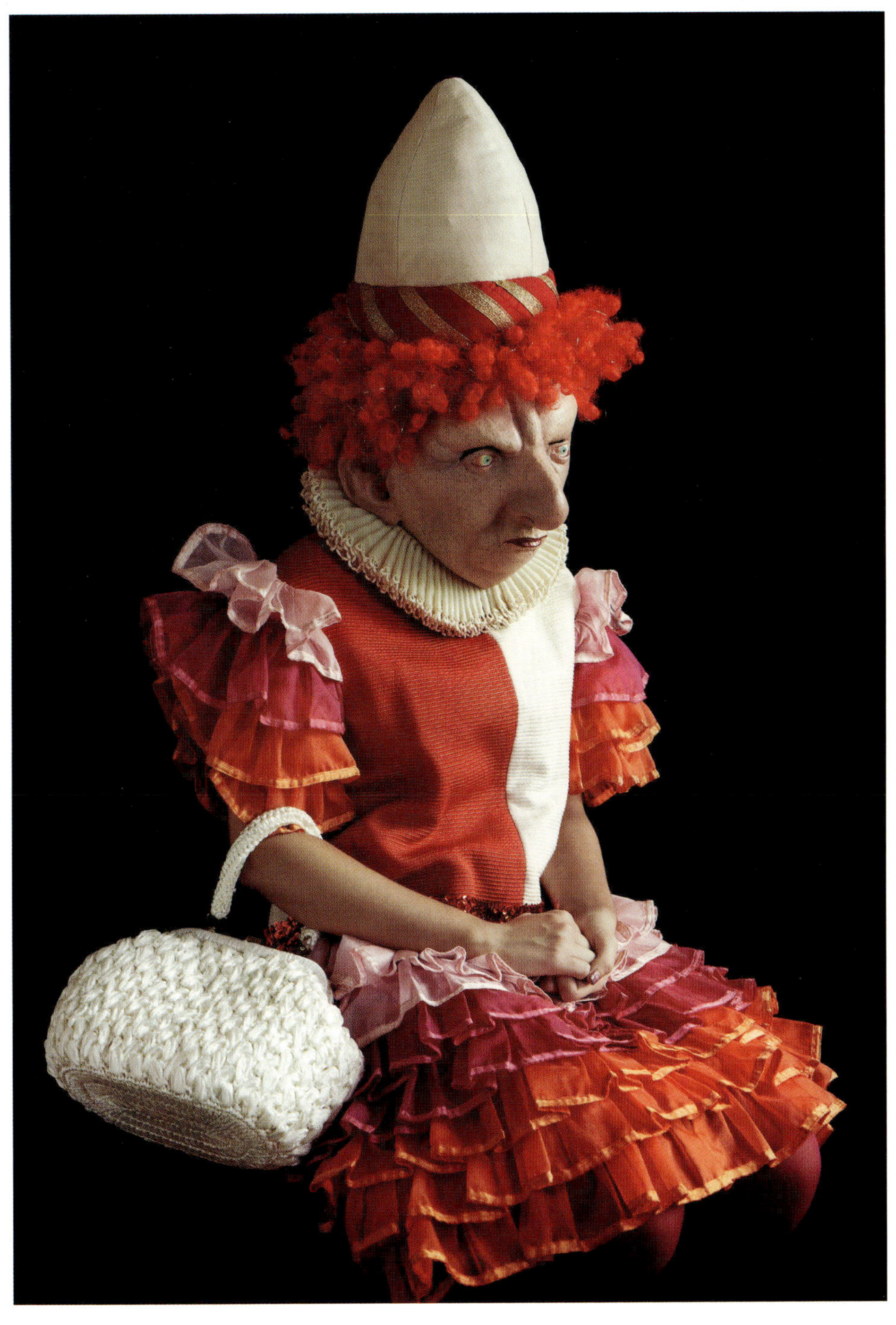

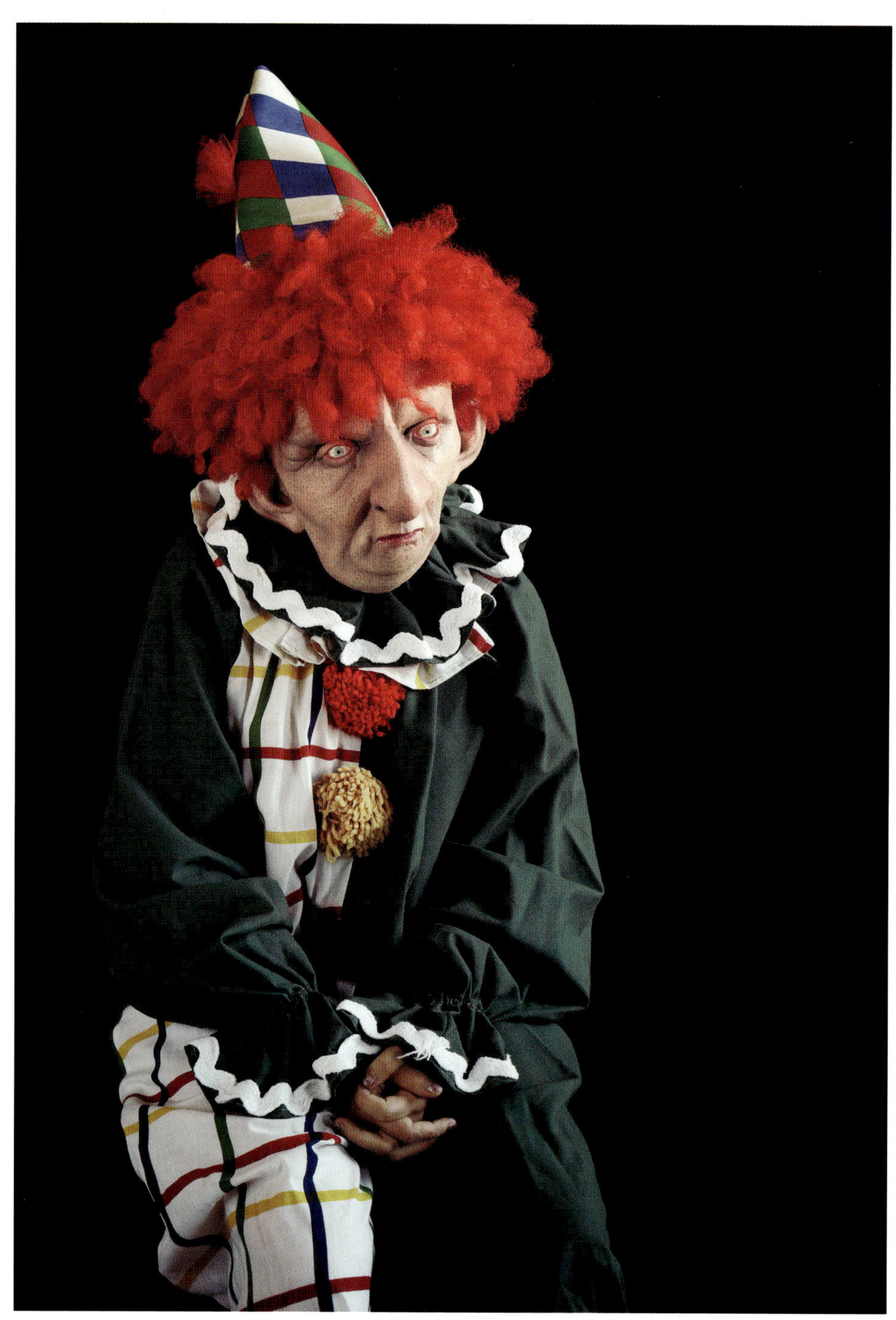

Somberness
2014

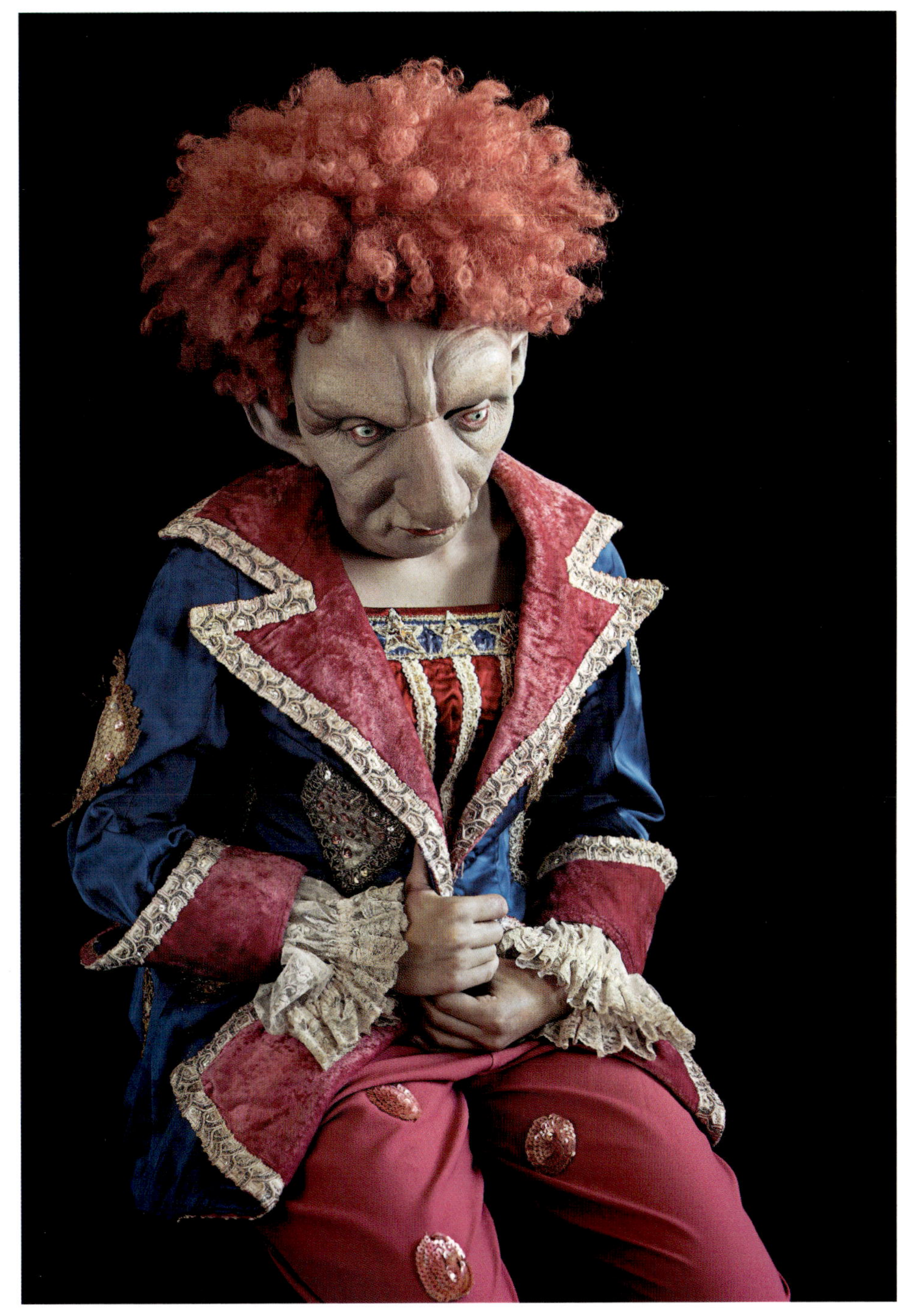

Grief
2014

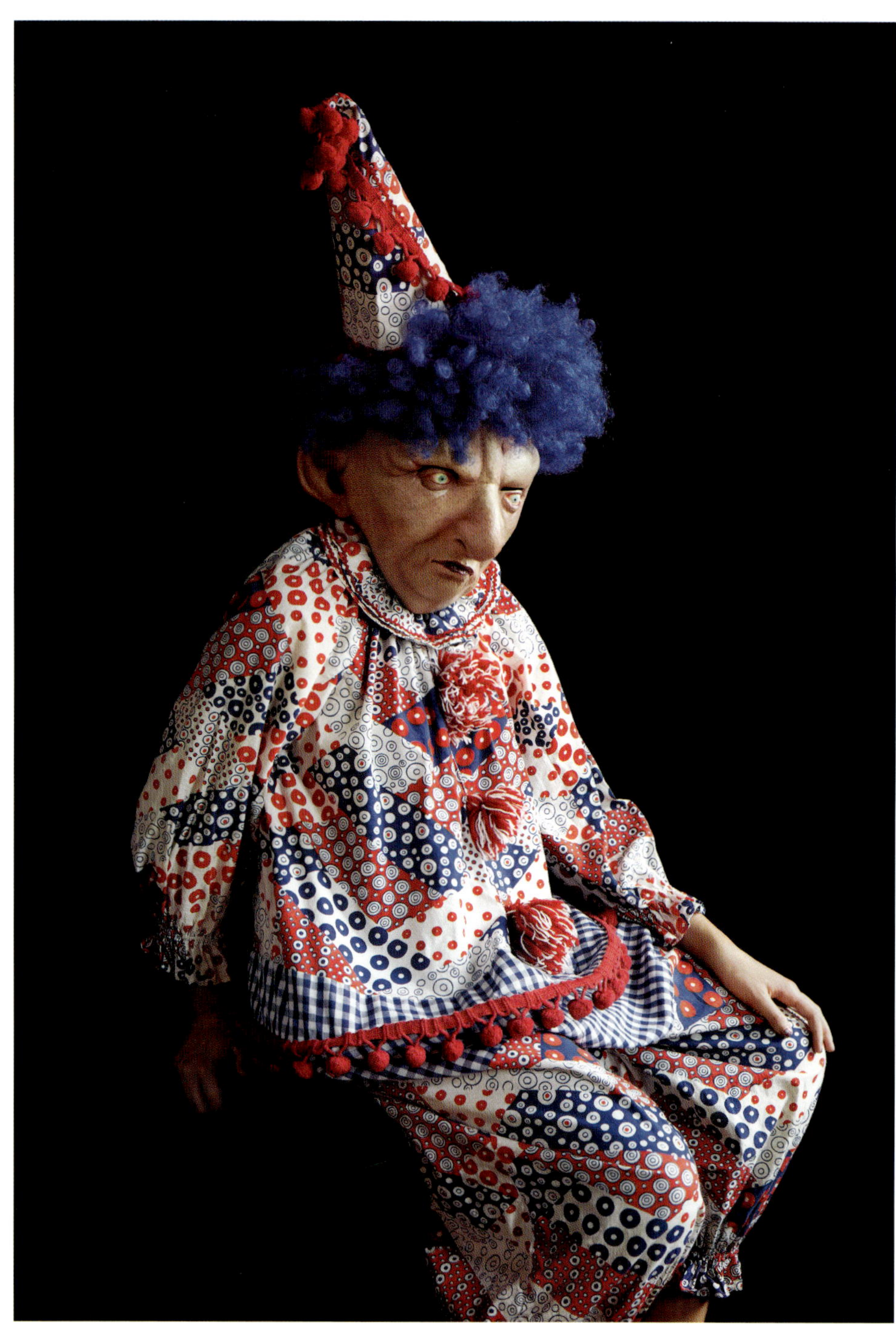

Despondency
2014

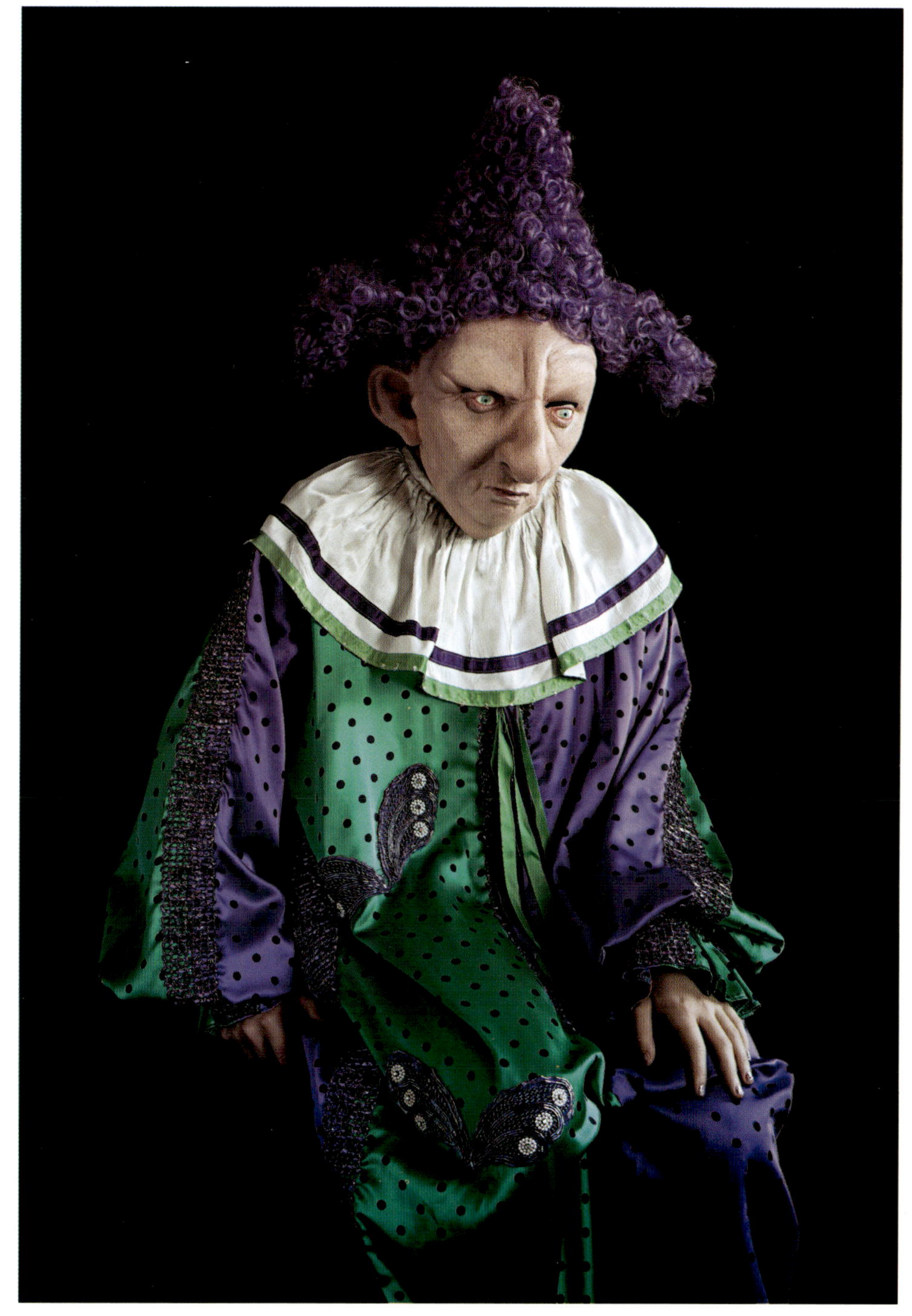

Sorrow
2014

Indian Brave
2002

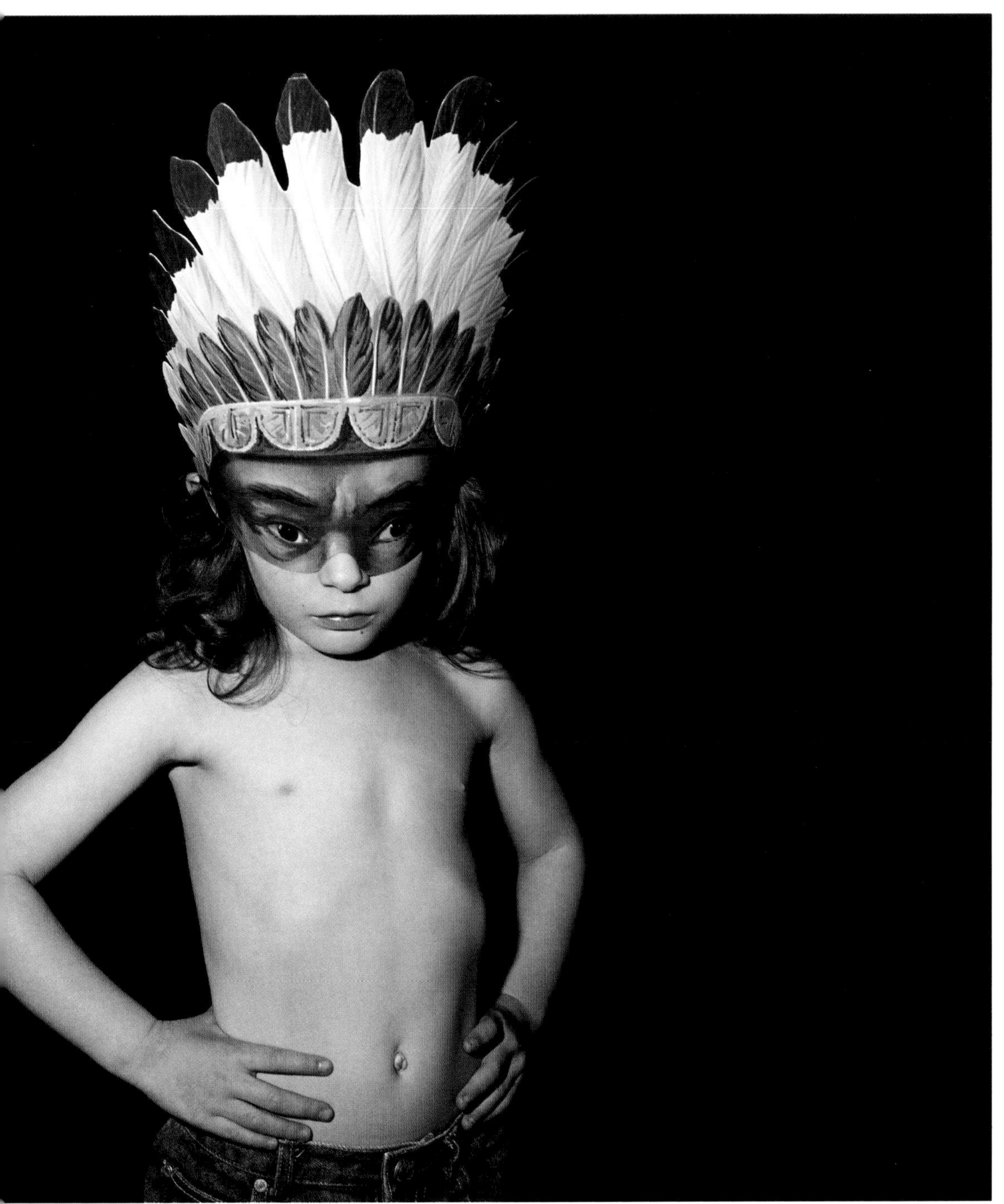

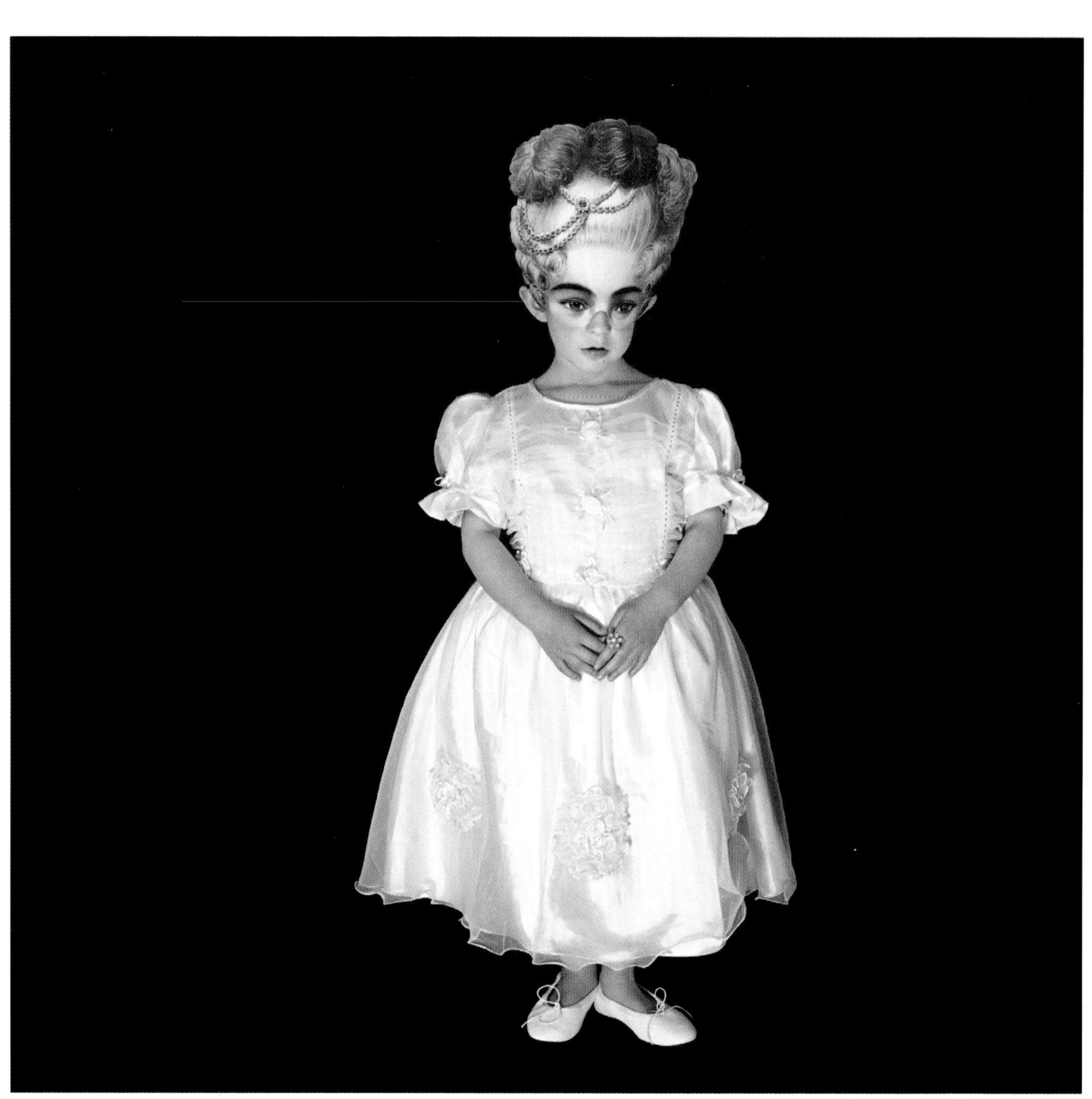

Court Beauty
2002

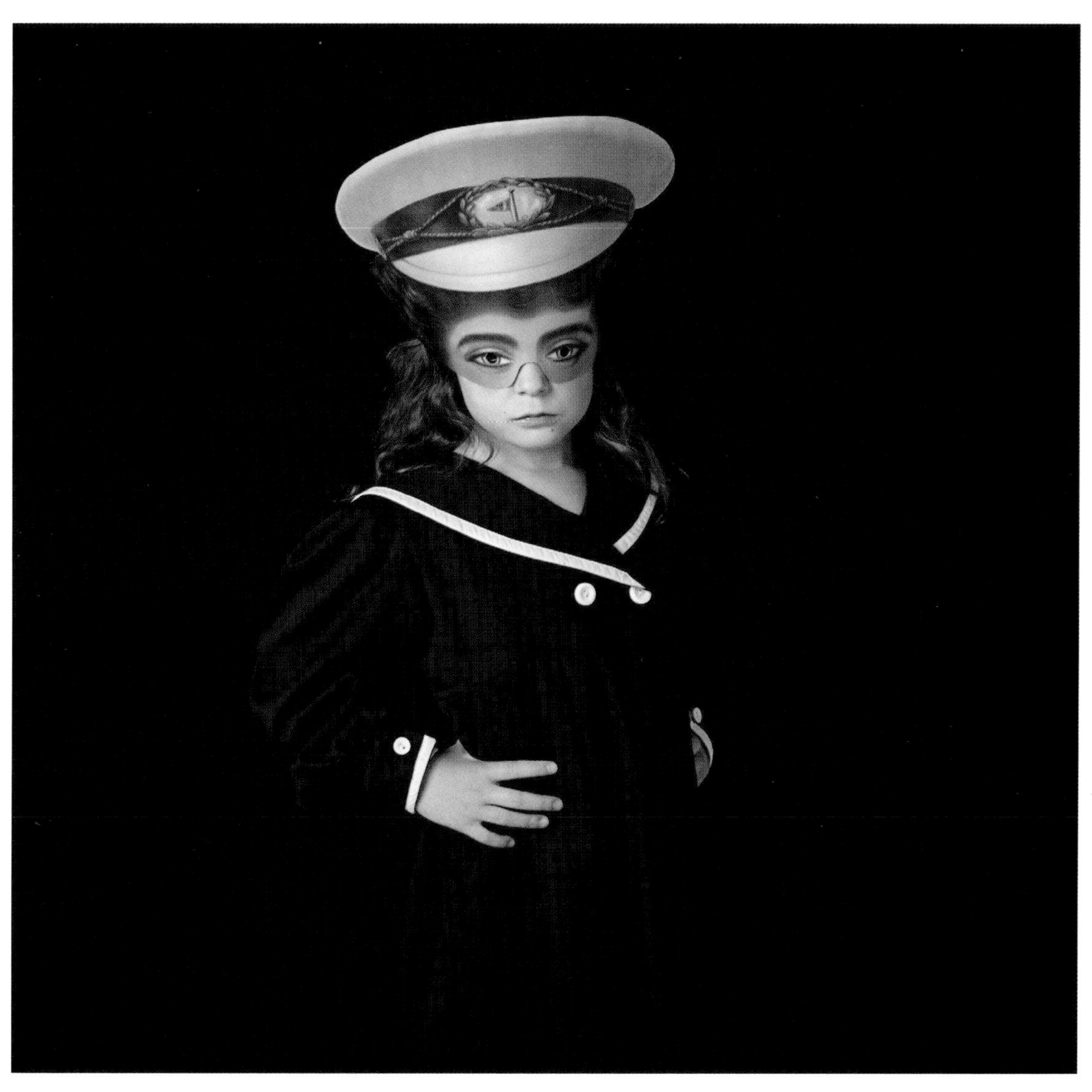

The Beauty of the High Seas
2002

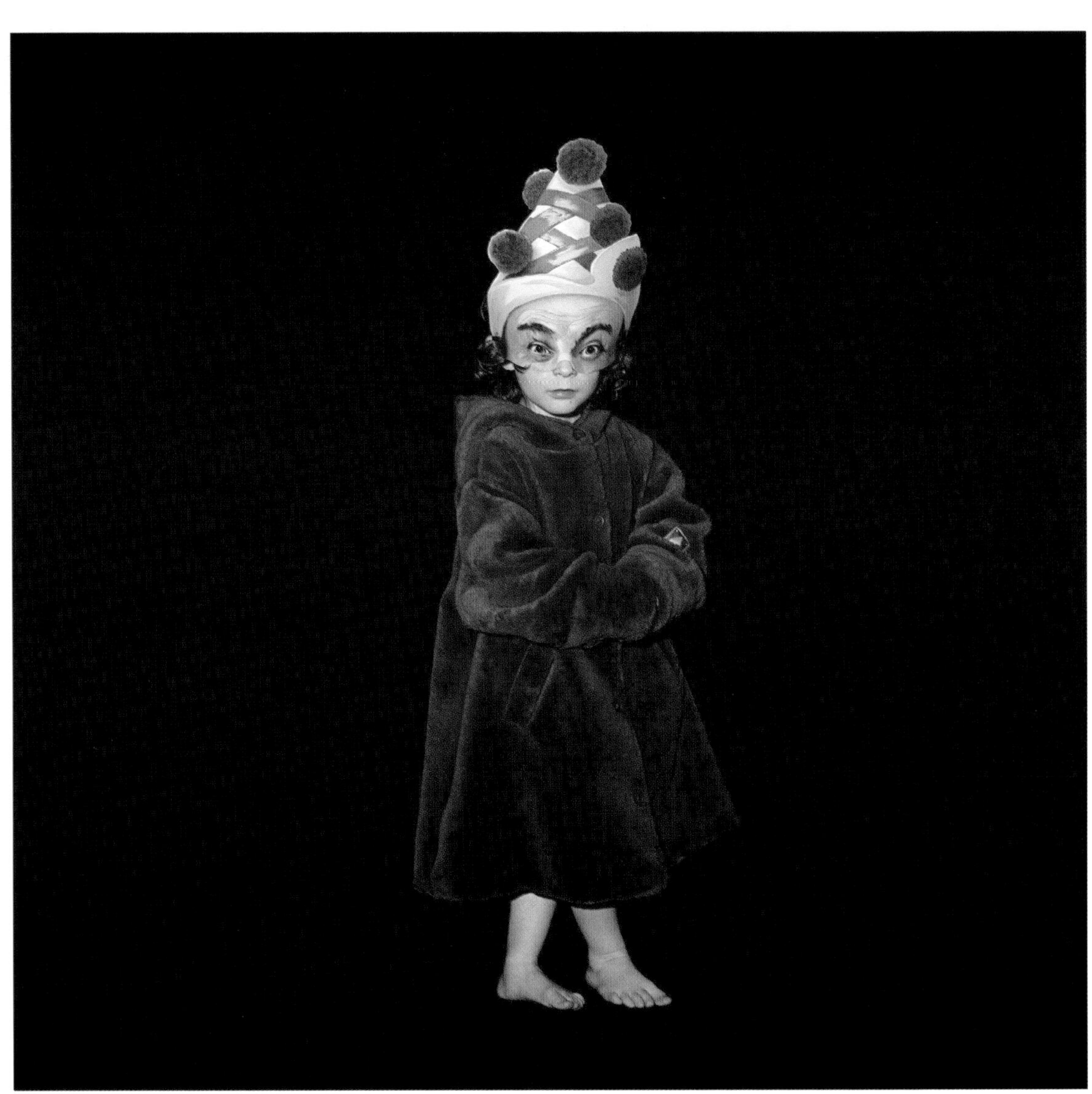

Winter Clown
2002

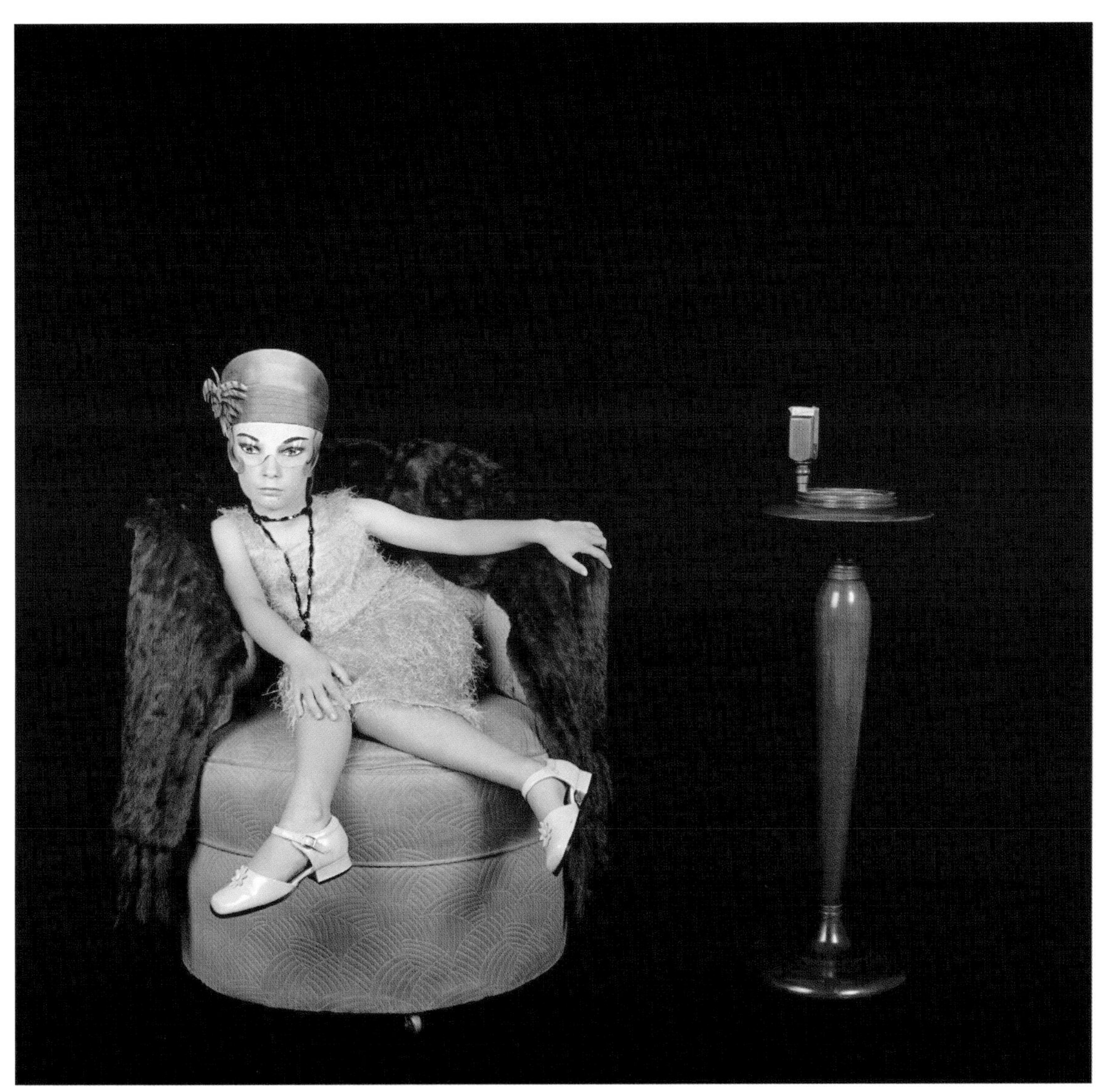

Gatsby Gal
2003

It's all about me
2016

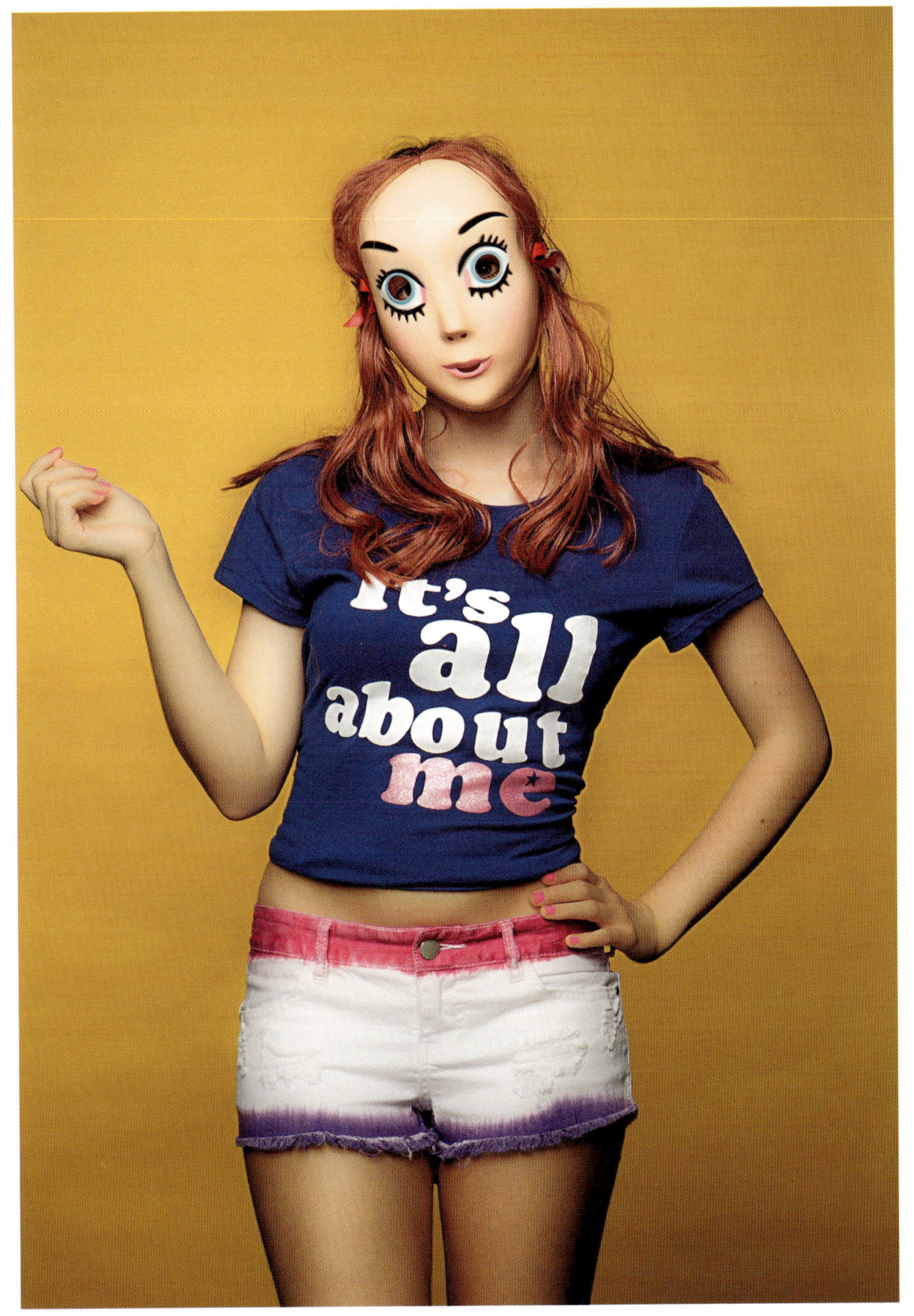
It's
all
about
me

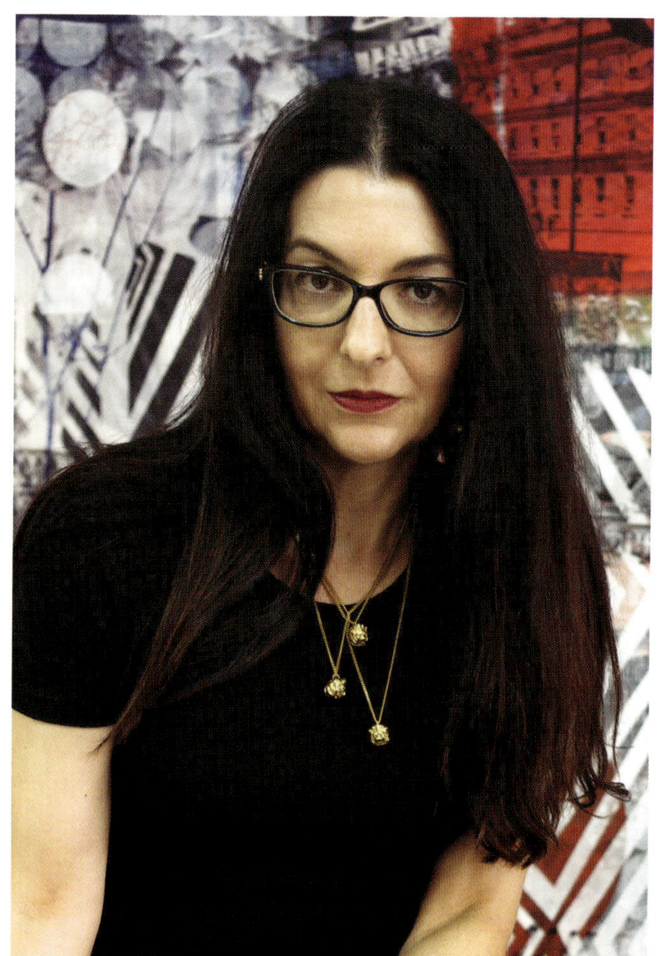

Image: Robert Nelson

TALES FROM THE DIORAMA

POLIXENI PAPAPETROU

Early in my daughter Olympia's life, around age three, a room in our house became a theatre. At first it was quite an abstract space, created by a large black velvet curtain hung against a wall. In its luxuriant darkness, Olympia would pose herself in any number of costumes that I had begun to collect or that my mother made for us. Olympia performed in front of the camera, in a space that had no background and no foreground: just her, perhaps some props, and an imaginary context proposed by her role. We saw it as a wonderful way to play together, to dress up and pretend. Children like to have their parents as an audience when they're performing. As Olympia had seen me working in the home studio photographing others, she asked me to 'photo her' and by doing so, I began a 17-year-long project engaging with the theme of childhood.

Slowly, the theatre evolved. Painted scenic backdrops were added, also quite luminous and suggestive. In those days, we had a carpeted floor, which caused the velvet and canvas to crumple and crease, so we constructed a wooden platform over it to make a little stage, a physical floor on which she performed. This theatre in a modest room became another world, suitable for making an image that reached beyond the reality that otherwise confined us. We could bring ourselves to a Chinese harbour, a riverbank in colonial times, an urban courtyard or a grove in Arcadia. The play-acting theatre transported us to ancestral times, to fictive or mythical times, symbolic times – but above all to the time of childhood, where stories are rehearsed in a vivid imagination that knows no boundaries.

The peculiar appeal of the studio theatre was not the fun that we had in it – because we could have had fun playing together in the playground – but that the fun created by the dress-ups yielded cultural and historical ideas where archetypes were formed: the ruler, the merchant, the official, the outsider, the poet, the animal, the recluse, the old, the child. Something about this engagement with history struck me as poetic. It was as if I had gained an intimacy with the immense space of time and cultures available to the imagination, mediated by the fantasy of a child.

The little theatre occupied my attention beyond the studio, as we would make excursions in search of props and clothes that might fit Olympia or my son, Solomon, and their friends. When I wanted to make work on a tragic Australian historical topic of the 'bush lost' children, I decided to take the studio into the landscape; but when we set out to make a photograph on the land, I would still look for a theatre, a flat stage, a platform that presented the actor or actors in a narrative context, and a backdrop that matched the proscenium arch of the camera's lens. These ideal theatrical locations were not always easy to find: my husband, Robert, also the driver, mused that it was easier for him to paint a scenic backdrop of three metres squared than to drive the family in search of the elusive theatre in nature. Over the years, I moved between the studio – with either its black curtain, the painted dioramas or other backdrops – and the landscape. For me, they both perfectly reflected the condition of childhood, as children can either see a world for themselves in their imagination or inhabit the real world that doesn't altogether belong to them. As much as I'd search for the theatre in nature, I also used my own childhood memories, recalling how children could invest the landscape with their games, their intuitions, their humorous resourcefulness and sense of adventure.

In the course of a lifetime, childhood is the shortest phase, yet it seems to have the most profound and lingering effect on us. Childhood experiences, which normally don't get recorded beyond infancy or birthdays, nevertheless survive mysteriously in the psyche and become a ghostly presence. When I started photographing Olympia at the age of three, it felt so natural and without any sense of exploitation. I realised that there was something about the images that I did not understand. Her presence felt enigmatic and puzzling. I decided to keep photographing her (and later in thematic ways) mainly as a way to memorialise her childhood years. Perhaps this was an unconscious attempt at experiencing childhood imagination and play, something I felt that I missed out on as a child of immigrants. Both my parents worked hard to create a future for their family and, as the eldest, I had the responsibility to care for my two younger siblings from the age of six. There was little time for dress-ups and play.

At a certain point I was criticised heavily by some people for photographing Olympia. Suddenly, I stood accused of being exploitative and a stage parent with a mouthy daughter. Throughout this period, it was Olympia who kept me motivated to keep working because she loved the pictures that we made together. At the age of eleven she appeared on national television to defend her pictures to the then prime minister of Australia who 'did not like these types of pictures'. Olympia was not troubled by this incident, which went global, and told me that she had something more important to worry about and that was my diagnosis of cancer.

From 2008, I decided to use masks in my work (which I had already used in *Phantomwise,* 2002–3), in part to conceal the identity of the children. Whether it was a reaction to the brouhaha caused by the prime minister I cannot say, but the masks suited an artistic purpose. I wanted the work to be about childhood identity in general rather than any one person. By covering the children's faces I was better able to address the transformation that childhood encounters: experimentation with identity, shedding one skin for another and shape-shifting. By concealing the personal identity of the children, I felt freer to make my work, but also to portray childhood in a more universal way. The masks make them magically odd, with uncanny multiple presences, perhaps proposing layers or levels of identity, like those on the surface and those in the unconscious.

In 2012 when my cancer became metastatic and life-threatening, my feelings about my work began to change. I was leaving Olympia, Solomon and all the children I photographed a legacy, a reminder of their youth that they could look back upon with happiness and pride. The pictures would simultaneously record their power to enter another being and to monumentalise their affair with the imagination. And even without these metaphorical ideas, I would hope that my photographs trigger a memory for viewers that reminds them of what it felt like to be a child navigating the world.

My children are now adults and I am heading towards the end of my life with terminal cancer. I cannot think of a more valid way to have lived the past 25 years than in tapping into that liminal and mysterious space of childhood. Inspiration did not come solely from my imagination, but rather from paying attention to theirs. You cannot claw back the years or the memories, but I would hope that my photographs of children memorialise those moments that may otherwise become buried in adult responsibilities. Those moments around the click of the shutter were thick with potential. First, they were moments in the diorama: constructed, performed, inhabited and connecting with another world through make-believe. Second, they were moments for receptiveness and reflection, moments that make analogies through art, inducing in viewers a sympathetic feeling that our lives are full of strata that are shared. And finally, the moment that is quintessentially shared is the awareness that we lose the moment itself, inevitably. Only photography and its sister-arts have the power to say, 'I once was and I was there.' I poetically existed.

ARTIST

Polixeni Papapetrou (1960–2018) was born in Melbourne to Greek immigrants. Her childhood experience of feeling like an outsider in a then predominantly Anglo-Saxon culture led her to question definitions of identity. Her sympathy for otherness remained a key element of her life and work. As a photomedia artist, her images explored the relationship between history, contemporary culture and identity. Her photographs of children dressing up, performing and wearing masks sought to explore the portrayal of childhood identity.

Her work has featured in over 50 solo exhibitions and over 100 group exhibitions in Australia, the USA, Asia and Europe. Survey exhibitions have been held at the Centre for Contemporary Photography, Melbourne, and the Australian Centre for Photography, Sydney. She exhibited in international photography festivals in Italy, Germany, Greece, France, Bratislava, the Netherlands, Colombia, China, Korea, Japan and Canada.

Papapetrou obtained a PhD from Monash University, a master's degree from RMIT University and bachelor's degrees in arts and law from the University of Melbourne. In 2009, she received the Josephine Ulrick and Win Schubert Photography Award and in 2017, she won the Bowness Photography Prize. She is survived by her two children and her husband, art critic and academic Robert Nelson.

ESSAYIST

Joanna Murray-Smith is a playwright, screenwriter, novelist and librettist. Her plays have been translated into many different languages and are performed all over the world, including on the West End and at the Royal National Theatre in London and on Broadway in New York. Joanna Murray-Smith is based in Melbourne and was a long-time friend of Polixeni Papapetrou.

SERIES EDITOR

Natalie King is an Australian curator, editor and arts leader with extensive expertise in international contemporary art, realising landmark projects in India, Indonesia, Japan, Korea, Singapore, Taiwan, Italy, Thailand and Vietnam. She is an Enterprise Professor at the Victorian College of the Arts, University of Melbourne.

In 2017, she was curator of *Tracey Moffatt: My Horizon*, Australian Pavilion at the 57th Venice Biennale, accompanied by a publication that she edited with Thames & Hudson.

She is widely published in arts media and is president of AICA-Australia (International Association of Art Critics). She is a member of the International Committee for Museums and Collections of Modern Art (CIMAM) and was a finalist in the AFR 100 Women of Influence 2018.

ARTIST'S ACKNOWLEDGEMENTS: 5 MARCH 2018

I would like to thank all the people who have supported me throughout my practice, beginning with the visionary instigators and contributors to the present volume: my publisher at Thames & Hudson, Kirsten Abbott, and the series editor, Natalie King, whose understanding of my images has resulted in such a beautiful layout. A sign of their editorial judgement was their faith in the writer Joanna Murray-Smith to produce such perceptive and poetic insights into my work, for which I am hugely grateful and touched.

The images on these pages have been lovingly honed and printed by my great artistic mentor, Dr Les Walkling, whom I thank not just for the look of the pictures but elements of their underlying logic and philosophy. I have been fortunate in having artistic and curatorial mentors, peers and fellow-travellers whom I also want to thank for countless conversations that have sustained me: the artists Euan Heng and Juan Davila, Patricia Piccinini, Stewart Russell, William Yang and Roy Chu, the poet Emmanuelle Guattari, the theorists Professors Anne Marsh, Nikos Papastergiadis and Rex Butler, Dr Susan Bright and Dr Adrian Martin, the curators Gael Newton, Victoria Lynn, Isobel Parker Philip, Tony Ellwood, Susan van Wyk and Maggie Finch, Dr Alasdair Foster, Naomi Cass and Shaune Lakin.

The photographs themselves rely on many participants, commencing with the actors, the young people who devoted many hours to a project that they not only understood but actively fashioned with their inspired gestures and presence. These players – if I can exploit the double meaning of gamer and thespian – deserve all my gratitude and admiration. Two of them are my own children, Olympia and Solomon Nelson; and certainly the whole family have been collaborators, including my mother, Effie, who made many costumes, my father for moral support and my husband, Robert Nelson, who helped with so many technical issues as my lighting engineer, driver and scene painter.

For 15 years, I have been supported by many commercial galleries and dealers who have operated with an altruistic exhibitions ethos, Kalli Rolfe and Nellie Castan in Melbourne, Stills Gallery and Michael Reid in Sydney, Michael Foley and Jenkins Johnson in New York, Letitia Delorme in Paris and Jarvis Dooney in Berlin.

And finally, I am indebted to all my other friends, who know who they are. My friendships have been sustaining for me as an artist because they have helped me discover who I am. My photography more often than not has caused me to question who I am; but my friends, simply by being my friends, have always reinforced my sense of identity and confidence to be myself in the studio and beyond.

First published in Australia in 2019
by Thames & Hudson Australia Pty Ltd
11 Central Boulevard, Portside Business Park
Port Melbourne, Victoria 3207
ABN: 72 004 751 964

www.thameshudson.com.au

22 21 20 19 5 4 3 2 1

Thames & Hudson Australia wishes to acknowledge that Aboriginal and Torres Strait Islander people are the first storytellers of this nation and the traditional custodians of the land on which we live and work. We acknowledge their continuing culture and pay respect to Elders past, present and future.

978 1 7607600 3 8

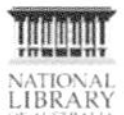

A catalogue record for this book is available from the National Library of Australia

Front cover:
Polixeni Papapetrou, *Heart*, 2016
Pigment ink print, 127.5 x 85 cm
Reproduced courtesy of the artist and Michael Reid Gallery, Sydney, and Jarvis Dooney Galerie, Berlin.

Design: Evi-O.Studio | Evi O & Rosie Whelan
Series editor: Natalie King
Printed and bound in Malaysia
by Times Offset (M) Sdn Bhd

Image credits

All works are pigment ink prints or C-type photographic prints, digitised by Dr Les Walkling.
Dimensions variable.
Images courtesy of the artist and Michael Reid Gallery, Sydney, and Jarvis Dooney Galerie, Berlin.

polixenipapapetrou.net